KIDS CAN MAKE MONEY TOO!

How Young People Can Succeed Financially

VADA LEE JONES

Calico Paws Publishing

Paws

Publishing

P.O. Box 2364
Menlo Park, CA 94026-2364

LIBRARY OF CONGRESS CATALOG CARD NUMBER: 87-71607

Jones, Vada Lee
   Kids Can Make Money, Too!
   How Young People Can Succeed Financially
   Includes Index.

ISBN 0-944104-00-2

Steve Lang: Cover design, San Jose, California
Holmes Typography: Book design, composition, page make-up and film, San Jose, California
Printing: Publishers Press, Salt Lake City, Utah

CONTENTS

PHOTOGRAPHIC CREDITS

All other pictures are the work of the author.

ABOUT THE AUTHOR

From an early age, Vada Lee was involved in money-making activities, sometimes for personal profit, often for charity, and frequently in partnership with her older brother, Philip.

When she was 8, Vada Lee delivered part of her brother's paper route. From ages 10 through 17, she raised chickens, ducks, rabbits, hamsters, white mice, guinea pigs, cats, opossums, and flying squirrels (more for fun than profit), and sold eggs and strawberries. Her father taught her how to build things and how to grow vegetables. When she was 6 years old, she had her own "Victory Garden" (toward the end of World War II).

In Grade School, she was president of the student body and received the Daughters of the American Revolution Junior American Citizenship Award.

In high school, Vada Lee was president of the Junior Honor Society, president of the Drama Club, reporter, then news editor for the school paper, and participated in many other activities, including chess, choir, cheer leading, music, and student government. She played left-wing on the girls' field hockey team, won awards for public speaking, and was appointed National Student Representative on the U.S. Treasury Savings Bond Committee in Washington, D.C.

She was a gung-ho salesman in Fairfax High School's annual magazine subscription drive, and sold ads for the school newspaper and yearbook.

After a successful 20-year career in real estate sales, including operating a one-woman real estate company, she now manages her own rental property, doing much of the maintenance herself.

She began making her own clothes after taking a sewing class in school. She learned crocheting from her grandmother, knitting from her mother, embroidery and quilting at church, and took piano lessons for several years.

She has had over 30 years of experience as a teacher and leader of children, teen-agers, and adults in Primary, Sunday School, Relief Society, and church youth programs, such as YWMIA, Girls' Summer Camp, and Seminary. She plays the piano for church, has written an award-winning musical drama, *Big Feet and an Empty Nest*, has coached basketball and volleyball, and has had many other exciting adventures in the service of others.

Vada Lee has written many children's stories, several of which have been published in *Jack And Jill, Highlights For Children,* and other children's magazines. This book draws on her vast and varied personal experience, and reflects her optimism for the future of today's youth.

The author and her brother were young entrepreneurs

To my parents, my children,
my grandchildren,

and to every young person
who reads this book and makes an effort
to apply the principles in it.

A Special Thanks
To My Husband, Claude,
whose integrity, humor, and good sense
bring a special quality to our lives,

and to his parents for teaching him honesty and
allowing him to develop money-managing skills
when he was a young boy.

ACKNOWLEDGEMENT

Sincere thanks and appreciation to . . .

. . . Claude Jones, Cindy Bay, Carol Sullwold, Cheryl Cromar, Chris Monson, Pat Norman, Libby Morris, Dolly Kyser, Ronald E. Plante, Al Hart, Edna Remson, Barbara J. Sutter, Norma Lyle, Bonny Pryor, Dave Wilson, Ida Vee Monson, and J. Harold Monson for their examples and personal encouragement, and for their contributions to this book by way of suggestions and evaluation,

. . . Bret Woodward for his humor, brainstorming, and technical assistance,

. . . Ian Monson for his proof-reading, editing, and positive energy,

. . . Buck and Julie Woodward, Russ and Rachel Woodward, Charles and Judy Hess, Philip R. Monson, J. Harold Monson, and Mary Jo Brimhall for their photography,

. . . Julie Jones for her photographic assistance,

. . . Daniel Woodward, Paul Woodward, Lamyra Nitra Jones, Lewis W. Scott III, Jeffery Hess, Jared Hess, Wells Brimhall, Joy Brimhall, Grant Brimhall, Shelley Brimhall, and Ryan Brimhall for their enterprising spirits and willingness to act as subjects for some of the photographs used in this book,

. . . Buck Woodward, Julie Woodward. Russ Woodward, Rachel Woodward, Janine Woodward, Bret Woodward, Terry Haines, Jennifer Jones-Scott, Arden Farey, and Philip R. Monson, whose pictures appear in this book,

. . . Marjorie Lin and her violin students, Peter Otte, Jeffery Hess, Herman Li, and Sara Aviel,

. . . Noni Aiken and her violin student, Sylvia Kong,

. . . Steve Lang for his artwork and valued suggestions as to the cover,

. . . and Bob Holmes for his helpful nature and for his assistance in preparing this book for publication.

WARNING – DISCLAIMER

The purpose of this book is to inform, inspire, amuse, and enlighten. It is not meant to be a substitute for professional advice and services—legal, accounting, or otherwise.

The author–publisher has used reasonable diligence in an effort to make this book factual and accurate. However, there might be mistakes in content, omissions, typographical errors, or other errors in the production or reproduction of this book.

Federal laws (including tax regulations) change, and state and local laws and ordinances vary (and change). Readers are encouraged to check with their parents, in the case of minors, with an attorney, accountant, or other appropriate professional, and with branches or departments of the Federal, State, and local governments, in order to make sure they are complying with the law before starting their business activities.

The author has not attempted to cover every aspect of each idea presented. Rather, it is her intention to stimulate the reader's desire to investigate carefully any of the suggestions briefly mentioned in this book, which are of particular interest to that reader.

When your work involves another person's house, yard, or possessions, you should be certain you are qualified, and you should be insured against physical or personal damage, loss, or accident.

There is risk of injury, when working with tools or animals. When working with other people's animals, there is the additional risk of unfamiliarity. The reader is advised to be particularly careful in these situations.

Neither the author nor Calico Paws Publishing will be responsible or liable for any problems, accidents, or losses sustained by any person, group, or organization as a result or alleged result, either directly or indirectly, of the contents of this book.

LABOR LAW

It is presumed that you will operate as an independent contractor when your decide to enter into any of the money-making activities suggested in this book.

Learn what an *independent contractor* is. find out the difference between an *independent contractor* and an *employee*. Go to the reference section of your local community library. Look up "minors," "children," and "independent contractor" in the general index to the several volumes of Law and Labor Law. Read the material that interests you.

There are many regulations about what children of various ages can do legally. These laws are designed to protect children from physical, emotional, and financial dangers and exploitation. Talk to your parents. Speak to an attorney.

If you plan to use machinery or power tools, be sure you have been carefully trained in the safe use of this equipment and that you are strong enough to handle it easily and safely.

INCOME TAX

Ask your parents to consult with their income tax accountant about any possible effects your activities might have on their taxes. Find out what kinds of income will be taxed at your parent's rate, even though it is your income. Note the differences (according to recent changes in the tax law) between *earned income* and *investment income*. Learn about *gross income* and *taxable income*.

The more you know about taxes, the better you can plan your financial course of action.

PART ONE

HOW TO SUCCEED

Part One is very important. If you skip it now and turn directly to Part Two: Some Ways To Make Money, come back to Part One and read it at least two times. Later, refer to it as needed.

CHAPTER 1

MONEY ISN'T EVERYTHING?

No, money is not everything and should not be the main focus of life. Other, more worthy concerns are health, education, service to others, marriage, raising happy and successful children, devotion to God and country, and making positive, productive contributions to society.

Without enough money to live, however, those worthy concerns take a back seat to *survival*.

Food, clothing, and shelter are basic needs and require money. Paying the bills is an urgent necessity for almost everyone, and the question, "Where will I get enough money to pay the bills?" usually takes up most of our time and energy.

It's nice to have some regular income from savings, investments, or enterprises other than wages earned by the hour. If you have this, your mind is able to work on other things, such as hobbies, creative ventures, expanding your talents, and having fun, plus the other worthy concerns listed earlier.

CHAPTER 2

MAKING MONEY ISN'T HAVING MONEY

Making money is important, and it is fun. It is a good beginning, but making money is not *having* money.

Everyone makes money. How many people have money left over after they pay their bills and buy groceries? Even people who make very good salaries still might not have money in the bank. I know lots of people who are like that, and probably you do, too.

There are only two ways to have money:
- **Make more than you spend,**
  or
- **Spend less than you make.**

As simple as this sounds, it is not easy for most people. For some, it is, and as you might guess, they are the ones with the money. They find it easy to make more than they spend *and* spend less than they make.

A few people seem to be born knowing how to manage money — like Alex P. Keaton on the television show, *Family Ties.*

If you are not a born money-manager, don't worry. What they do naturally, you can learn. If you are one of the lucky few, you are probably eager to improve your natural skill. Even Alex P. Keaton is still learning new ways to make and manage money.

HERE ARE TWELVE WAYS
TO MANAGE YOUR MONEY BETTER

1. SPEND WISELY

First, buy only what you need. If you are just starting out, you should learn how to reduce your needs well below your income. This doesn't mean you should not dream, plan, and set goals. By all means, dream. Let the challenge of building your financial security satisfy your urge to spend money.

The less money one has, the greater the compulsion to spend it. When television first came on the market, it was a major investment. I was in the seventh grade, living in a rural community in Virginia, near Washington D.C. We could tell by the antennas, who had just bought a television set. The first homes to have TV were the smallest little shacks. I am not exaggerating: they were little shacks. As we rode to school on the school bus, we could see new antennas each day. This made a deep impression on me.

Classmates from the poorest homes always had spending money. They would go across the street during recess and buy junk food at Tony's Market. They got their kicks spending money; I got mine saving it and investing in United States Savings Bonds. Back then, you could buy ten-cent savings stamps, glue them in a booklet, and turn that in for a twenty-five-dollar bond when it was full. (I bought my first house with these Savings Bonds, at age 20.)

I still see the same addiction to spending among many people in California, where I live now. When I was manager and part-owner of a small apartment building just barely on the right side of the tracks, I learned to collect the rent on payday—before the money was gone.

If you must buy something, look at the ads and compare prices. If you can buy the same item for less at a certain store and the guarantee is the same, why pay more?

Compare food prices. Find a store where prices are the lowest and go there most of the time, provided it is clean. It's no bargain, if you bring home mealy-bugs in your cereal. Also, avoid dented canned goods and out-dated products.

Shop the specials. Buy things when they are on sale.

Grocery stores feature different items each week at special prices. Most grocery ads appear in the local newspaper on the same day, so it is easy to compare prices.

There are seasonal sales for clothes, as well as other special sales throughout the year.

Learn about discount stores in your area. Warehouse outlets, manufacturers' outlets, and wholesale outlets are often good places to shop.

A well-to-do woman I know once said she didn't know anyone who paid full-price for anything. That must be an exaggeration, but obviously *she* never did.

If you aren't shopping for groceries or clothes now because of your age, you might want to help your parents save money. It's good practice for you and at the same time helpful to them. This, by the way, could be one of your projects to earn money. Your parents could pay you a percentage of the money you help them save.

Caution: Don't buy merchandise you don't need, just because it is on sale. The stores are hoping you will do just that. Resist the temptation. Try not to buy on impulse, unless you accidentally find something you really need. It's easy to make a purchase that seems like a good idea when you are in the store, only to get home and realize it was a mistake. Almost everyone has this problem. Train yourself to know the difference between a "good find" and a "good-for-nothing find."

2. SAVE REGULARLY

Now that you are controlling your spending, you are in a good position to start saving regularly. This should be the first thing you do after paying any bills you owe. Pay *yourself* by placing at least ten or twenty percent of your earnings into a savings account.

Regular saving is so obvious and so simple that most people never get around to doing it. When you look at the following

Shop for a savings account—start early

tables, notice the clear advantage of beginning your savings program as soon as possible. Also notice interest compounded daily, versus monthly.

"Compounding" interest daily or monthly means the interest is figured and credited to your account once each day or once each month. The next day or month, interest is figured again on your investment plus the interest for yesterday or last month, and so on.

TABLE #1: 5% Interest Compounded Daily*

Invest	Balance After				
Monthly	5 yrs	10 yrs	15 yrs	20 yrs	25 yrs
$ 30	2,053	4,698	8,106	12,498	18,156
100	6,843	15,660	27,021	41,659	60,519
300	20,529	46,980	81,063	124,977	181,557

*Using a 360-day year

TABLE #2: 5% Interest Compounded Monthly

Invest	Balance After				
Monthly	5 yrs	10 yrs	15 yrs	20 yrs	25 yrs
$ 30	2,040	4,658	8,019	12,331	17,865
100	6,801	15,528	26,729	41,103	59,551
300	20,402	46,585	80,187	123,310	178,653

As you can see, the same monthly investment gives you a better return when the interest is compounded daily, instead of monthly.

You might also expect a higher interest rate to make a difference. The next two tables show what happens when the interest paid is 10%.

TABLE #3: 10% Interest Compounded Daily*

Invest	Balance After				
Monthly	5 yrs	10 yrs	15 yrs	20 yrs	25 yrs
$ 30	2,354	6,262	12,749	23,518	41,396
100	7,846	20,872	42,496	78,393	137,986
300	23,539	62,616	127,488	235,179	413,958

TABLE #4: 10% Interest Compounded Monthly

Invest	Balance After				
Monthly	5 yrs	10 yrs	15 yrs	20 yrs	25 yrs
$ 30	2,323	6,145	12,434	22,781	39,805
100	7,744	20,485	41,447	75,937	132,683
300	23,231	61,454	124,341	227,811	398,050

*Using a 360-day year

It is important to look for a savings account that pays the best interest. Over several years, the extra interest makes a big difference. If you invest $100 per month at 5% interest compounded daily, after 25 years you will have $60,519 (Table #1.) The same investment at 10% interest yields $137,986 after 25 years (Table #3.)

The single most important thing to remember is to deposit money into your account regularly, starting *now*. Every time you get paid, pay yourself.

> *Caution:* When you are shopping around for the best interest rates and terms, be sure to consider only banks or savings and loans that are insured. Usually there is a notice of insurance on the window or in another place where you can see it. If you don't see it, ask.
>
> Don't make the mistake of trying to get a higher interest rate at an uninsured institution. I did that once and lost my money when the savings and loan went bankrupt.
>
> Each account can be insured only up to a certain dollar amount. Find out what that is, and when you reach the limit, move some of your money to a different institution.

There are many kinds of accounts that pay interest and can be considered savings accounts. Some examples are: Regular Savings, Market Interest, Checking-Savings, Certificates of Deposit (known as CD's), Business Savings, Retirement Savings, and many more. In order to attract business, banks keep inventing new types of accounts with fancy names.

A Money-Market Fund can be used as a savings account. It usually pays a higher interest rate than a regular savings account, but you have to deposit more money to open the account.

Before you look for a savings account, you should ask yourself,

• What is my goal? (How much money?)

• How soon will I need the money?

• Do I want to have access to the money before my goal is reached? (Perhaps just to move it to a different account, in order to earn a higher rate of interest.)

• Am I interested in a free safe deposit box, free traveler's checks, free cashier's checks, or other free services?

Every account is different, but the main thing is to find a way to save and *leave the money there.* Beware of the "Put 'n Take" method of saving, where you put it in, then take it out.

If you get into the habit of taking money out of your savings account, it will not be there when you are ready to use it for college or some other important personal goal. Stick to your plan. Use the money to accomplish your LONG-TERM goal. Don't allow yourself even to *think* of dipping into your savings for small emergencies. Pretend you don't have it or can't get at it. Think of your goal often, and enjoy the secure feeling of knowing you will have the money to carry out your plan.

Look for an account that allows you to:

• Make regular deposits.

• Earn a good interest rate.

• Take out the money at the right time, with no penalty.

• Defer taxes, if taxes are a problem for you.

• Sleep, knowing your money is safe.

3. HAVE A PERSONAL CHECKING ACCOUNT, PLUS A SEPARATE CHECKING ACCOUNT FOR YOUR BUSINESS

The easiest way to keep good records is to have a personal checking account and another one for your business. This prevents problems with the Internal Revenue Service (IRS) and helps you see exactly how your business is doing.

Even though you are not an adult, you can still have a checking account, if you have some money to put in it. As a matter of policy, the bank might require one of your parents to be on the account with you. They worry about children being able to handle checking accounts, because a lot of adults can't.

One reason adults are unable to manage their checking accounts is because they never learned this when they were children. The time to learn important things like multiplication tables and how to use checking accounts is when you are young.

It's easier that way. You don't forget things you learn in your youth.

Shopping for a checking account means going to banks and savings and loans just as you do when you are looking for the right savings account. However, in this case it is important for your checking account to be close and convenient, since you will be going there often.

Find out what hours they are open. Can you go there during those hours? Are they open on Saturday? Do they have an "Automatic Teller" outside so you can use it any time of the day or night? Actually, it is best to go into the bank to conduct your business, if possible. That way they will get to know you.

My husband has been banking at a certain bank for about eighteen years. Because he uses the automatic teller outside most of the time, the tellers working in the bank don't know him. When he tried to deposit a pay check that was made out to someone else and signed over to him, the teller would not accept it. Had she recognized him as a good customer, he would not have had any trouble.

The next question to ask is whether the bank's checks clear locally, or whether they have to go through a home office in another state. If they don't clear in your state, you will occasionally have trouble using your checks or cashier's checks from that bank. Escrow companies in California will not accept cashier's checks that don't clear in-state, unless you allow extra time for them to clear. This is a fairly recent problem, and it causes some major difficulties for people trying to buy or refinance property.

If you are not planning to buy a house yet, you soon will. Unless you want to change banks then, you will do well to think about this now.

NOTE: A "cashier's check" is a check written by the bank and guaranteed by them to be good. This used to be the same as actual dollar bills, with no waiting period required for the check to clear. Now, in California at least, these checks only work that way if they don't have to leave the state to clear.

Next, try to find a checking account with no service charge, no minimum balance required, and one that pays interest. Sometimes there is a service charge or no interest paid, if the balance falls below a certain amount. Try to find an account that is both free and pays interest, no matter what the balance is. From time to time, banks and savings and loans have special promotions when such accounts are offered. Open two. One you will use for your business, the other you will use for your personal needs.

If you can't find a free account, get one with the least minimum balance required.

Some banks offer good terms long enough to get your business, then change the terms later. Others continue to honor the original agreement, even if they stop offering those terms for new accounts. Ask around. My experience with First Interstate and Eureka Federal Savings in California has been good on that score so far.

When you go into a bank or savings and loan, or to see a stock broker, try not to worry about being young, and don't be afraid to admit you are a beginner.

If you have some good questions ready (write them down), you might even surprise some people with what you already know. Be careful not to give the impression that you know more than you do, or you might not understand what is said next. If someone laughs at you or says your expectations are impossible, don't worry. It might be impossible there, but not necessarily everywhere.

You should be treated with courtesy. If you are treated any other way, someone will risk losing your present business as well as your future business, when you are older.

It would be good to go alone, but it is all right to go with a parent or some other adult, at least the first time. If you take an adult with you, be sure they understand that you are shopping and don't want to open an account at the first place you visit. Let them know what you are looking for in an account. They might know where to begin looking, and they might have some other useful ideas to offer you.

If your parents are good, long-time customers at a particular bank, you might be able to get favorable terms there because of that. It's nice to start out completely on your own, but if you do

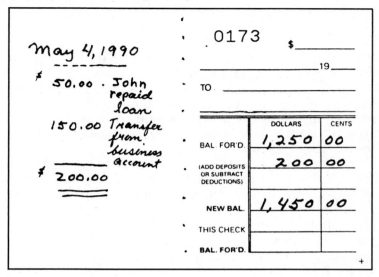

Figure #1: Deposits

accept special treatment based on your parents' reputation, you will want to be as responsible as they are. For instance, NEVER OVERDRAW YOUR ACCOUNT by trying to take out more money than you put in.

When you open your account, you will have to deposit some money in it and choose your checks. When it comes to checks, not only do I prefer "end-stubs," but I absolutely must have them. I never have been able to use the flat, wallet style, where the stub is separate from the checks. Nor can I use the "top-stub" style very well. I don't see how anyone can, but obviously lots of people do.

Let me explain how you can use the end-stub checkbook. First, get the large book with three checks (and stubs) on a page. This gives you more room on the backs of the stubs to make important notations. It might cost more than other styles, but it is worth it.

Deposits

When you make a deposit, you can write in the blank space on the left (opposite the stubs), which is the reverse side of the previous three stubs. Write the date first. Under that, write the amount of each item deposited and the source of the money. Then, add up all the items to get a total. This total goes on the stub at the right, under "deposits" and is added to the "balance forward." (See Figure #1.)

This way, every deposit is dated, itemized, and identified. Always do this, no matter what the source of the deposit. It's an easy way to have a complete record, and enables you to track your money.

Not only is this important for your own records, but it is a *must* for the IRS. If you take money from one account and deposit it in another, that is not taxable income. Gifts are not taxable, if they are under the limit set by the Internal Revenue Code and the Gift Tax Laws. Borrowed money is not taxable. If you lend money to someone else, and they pay you back, that is not taxable. (However, *interest* earned and collected on money you lend *is taxable*). When someone reimburses you for an item you purchased for them, that is not taxable.

By labeling each deposit, you can prove what it is, and pay taxes only on actual income. Otherwise, the IRS might argue that the unlabeled deposit is taxable income.

Every time you make a deposit, have the teller record it in a little deposit book. This is the easiest way to double-check, if you think you have forgotten to record a deposit in your checkbook, or if you think you have deposited a check in the wrong account. Some banks will only give you a deposit book if you ask for it. Other banks won't use the book at all, because they are afraid to give you two receipts for the same deposit. (The computer prints out a receipt.) In this case, you can find or make your own book and keep it yourself. Or you can keep every loose receipt in an envelope with your checkbook (more haphazard).

Writing checks

Use the correct date when you write a check.

Sooner or later, someone will try to talk you into putting a future

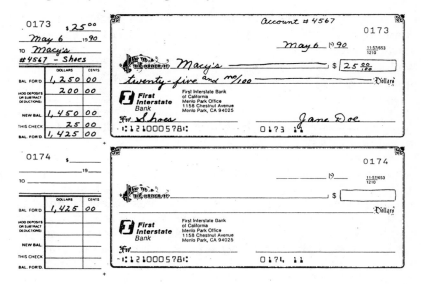

Figure #2: Writing Checks

date on a check as a form of money-back guarantee, or because you do not yet have enough money in your account to cover the check. This person will tell you that you will have time to deposit the money before the date on the check. There will be some reason why they must have the check at that time, but they will promise *not to deposit it* until the date you have written on it.

Often, they *will deposit the check* by accident or by design. The check will either be refused at the bank as it should be (because of the improper date), or it will be accepted and processed by mistake. Then, if you don't have enough money in your account, one of two things will happen: the check will bounce, or it will be paid and cause other checks you have written to bounce. Either way will cost you money in penalty fees, and your checking account will be a mess.

Don't risk it. Use the correct date on your checks.

Write the number of the invoice or your account number at the very top of the right-hand side of the check. (See Figure #2.)

At the bottom of the check next to, "For_____," explain the payment. (See Figure #2.)

On the stub to the immediate left of that check, enter the amount of the check, the date, to whom it is written, the explanation, and the account number. Each stub is numbered to match the attached check. Subtract the amount from your balance and carry the new reduced balance forward to the top of the next stub. (See Figure #2.)

Always fill in the stub as you write the check (preferably *before* you write the check). Make certain the stub and check match in every detail.

If you add and subtract as you go along, you will always know your balance. This is the key to keeping a positive balance in your account.

Some people (I know several) try to guess their balance by asking the teller at the bank what it is. There is no way the bank can know how many checks you have written that have not yet been subtracted from your account. A balance figure from the bank is practically meaningless. If you keep asking for it, the only thing it will mean is that you don't have any idea what you are doing.

NOTE: Use a pen, not a pencil. This is both for writing checks and filling in your stubs. If you discover a mistake on your stubs, don't try to erase. Just make an adjustment to your current balance and refer it back to the mistake. I use red ink for corrections. It prevents confusion.

If you don't want to carry your checkbook with you (especially the large three-check binder type), you can carry one or two checks and a check-sized piece of paper on which you write down the number of the check and all the stub information every time you use a loose check. Also, have your balance written on the paper, so you will not write a check for more than you have in the account. Carry this paper and the checks in a safe place, such as your wallet. When you get home, make the entry in your checkbook.

The wallet-style checkbook has one advantage — you can carry it easily in purse or pocket. This seems like a wonderful convenience, but it is actually a potential hazard. If you carry your checkbook with you, it can easily be lost or stolen. This would be a major disaster. Not only will you be worrying about someone trying to use your checks, but you will have lost all the records on your check stubs.

Caution: NEVER OVERDRAW YOUR BANK ACCOUNT by writing checks for more than your balance. This would harm your credit. The bank charges a penalty when it happens, and could close your account, if you do it often.

To prevent overdrafts, keep your balance above $100, $500, $1,000, or more, depending on the amount of money you have flowing through your checking account. If you are dealing in dollars, $100 will do. If you are making and spending thousands of dollars, you should keep a much larger reserve.

NOTE: If you make a mistake while writing a check, tear out the signature line, but don't throw away the check. Keep it, so you can account for all checks. I would stable it to the stub. This is important to you and possibly to the IRS.

Reconciliation

When you "reconcile" your balance with the bank statement each month, you can do it on the blank sides of the end stubs opposite the last check to clear that month.

First, as a heading write, "Reconciliation to May 21, 1990," or the last date of the period covered by the statement. Then write the balance you have in your checkbook after subtracting the last check to clear (or come back). Add the amounts of any checks that have not yet cleared, if they were written during the period you are reconciling. (Arrange the returned checks in numerical order and check them off on each stub. Double-check the amount of each check as you do this, and check them off on the statement, to see if you have them all. On the stubs, circle the numbers of checks that have not cleared.)

Next, add the interest credited to your account, and enter it in your checkbook. In your reconciliation, show the number of the check stub where you enter the interest, and refer the entry back to the location of the reconciliation by the number of the stub to which you are reconciling. Do this with all adjustments you make in your checkbook.

Check the deposits listed on the statement against those entered in your checkbook. On your reconciliation, subtract recent deposits that were not on the statement, if they are included in the balance you are verifying.

If there are any charges by the bank, such as for new checks, subtract this and also enter the charge in your checkbook. Subtract it from your current balance. (See Figure #3.)

The answer you now have in your reconciliation should be the same as the balance shown on the bank statement. If so, circle and check it on the bank statement, and in the reconciliation. On the stub, circle and check the "balance forward" verified by the reconciliation. (See Figure #3.)

Remember, this is not your current balance. It is simply the balance you had at the time the bank statement was prepared. Also note that the balance on the bank statement does not reflect checks that have not yet cleared, including recent checks you have written, nor does it reflect recent deposits you have made.

If your answer does not match the balance on the bank statement, you have probably made a mistake in your arithmetic, or forgotten to add or subtract something in your reconciliation. If the arithmetic in your reconciliation seems to be correct, find the difference between the bank's answer and yours. If your answer is more, divide the difference by 2. Look for a check for that exact amount. If there is one, you could have added the amount of that check to your balance, instead of subtracting it.

If your answer is less than the bank's, do the same thing to see if you subtracted a deposit, instead of adding it.

If that doesn't work, look for other mistakes in your arithmetic. When you find your mistake, make the correction on the

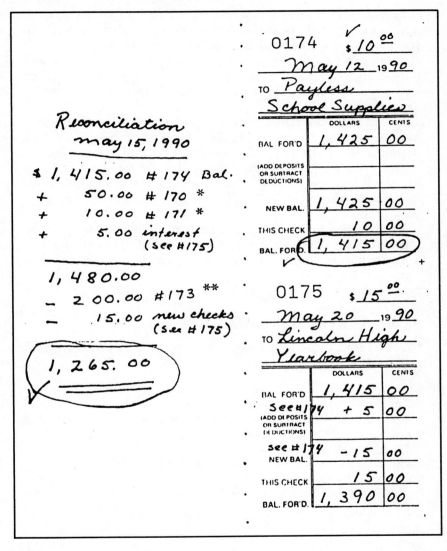

Reconciliation
may 15, 1990

$ 1, 415.00 # 174 Bal.
+   50.00 # 170 *
+   10.00 # 171 *
+   5.00 interest
                  (see #175)

1, 480.00
- 2 00.00 #173 **
-    15.00 new checks
                  (see #175)

1, 265. 00

0174 $ 10 00
May 12 19 90
TO Payless
School Supplies

	DOLLARS	CENTS
BAL. FOR'D	1, 425	00
(ADD DEPOSITS OR SUBTRACT DEDUCTIONS)		
NEW BAL.	1, 425	00
THIS CHECK	10	00
BAL. FOR'D.	1, 415	00

0175 $ 15 00
May 20 19 90
TO Lincoln High
Yearbook

	DOLLARS	CENTS
BAL. FOR'D	1, 415	00
See #174 (ADD DEPOSITS OR SUBTRACT DEDUCTIONS)	+ 5	00
see #174 NEW BAL.	- 15	00
THIS CHECK	15	00
BAL. FOR'D.	1, 390	00

*   Uncleared check
** Uncleared deposit

Figure #3: Reconciliation

stub where you show your last balance. Don't forget to write the number of the stub reconciled and the number of the stub where you found a mistake, and vice versa.

It doesn't happen very often, but sometimes the bank will have made a mistake. You can usually tell right away if they have, because the kinds of mistakes made by a bank are often dramatic.

Two months in a row, my bank deposited large sums of money into my account that were intended for another account with a similar number. One month it was $50,000, and the next month it was $70,000. Naturally, the other customer complained about his missing money, but the bank was unable to identify their mistake on their own. When I informed them of it, they were very relieved (twice).

By the third month, they had corrected the computer or the other person's deposit slips, and my windfall deposits stopped.

You can write other notes to yourself on the left-hand side of the stubs, but it is best not to clutter this space too much, or you won't have room to do your reconciliations.

SUMMARY OF THE CHECKBOOK:

- Get a large, end-stub style checkbook with three checks and stubs to a page.

Deposits:

- Opposite the stub, write the date of the deposit, the amount of each item, and the source of the money.

- Enter the total deposit on the stub, next to "Deposits."

- Add deposits to your "Balance Forward."

- Record the deposit in a small deposit book.

Writing checks:

- First, fill in the stub with all the information that will appear on the check, including account number and explanation.

- (Use a pen, not a pencil.)

- Always write the correct date on the check and stub.

- Write the account number or the invoice number at the top of the right-hand side of the check.

- Fill in the name of the person you are paying, next to, "Pay to the order of."

- Write the amount of the check in numbers.

- Write out the amount of the check in words.

- State what the payment is for, next to "For" (shoes, school supplies, etc.).

- Sign the check.

Reconciling to your bank statement:

- Arrange the cleared checks in numerical sequence.

- Verify the amount of each check against the bank statement and your checkbook, and check them off.

- On your stubs, circle the numbers of checks that have not cleared.

- Verify the deposits listed in the bank statement against those entered in your checkbook. Put a check-mark by them.

- If there are mistakes, make corrections on your current stub. Do not erase or change the error, simply cross-reference it to the location of the correction, using the number of the stub.

- Reconcile on the blank side of the end-stubs.

- Write, "Reconciliation to _____." Use the last date included in the bank statement.

- Under that, write the balance in your checkbook as of the last check included in the bank statement.

- Under that, add the amounts of any checks written earlier that have not yet cleared.

• Add interest credited to your account by the bank. Enter this also in your checkbook on your current stub, and cross-reference.

• Subtract the amounts of deposits that have not cleared, but have been included in the balance you are verifying from your checkbook.

• Subtract any bank charges listed on your statement, such as a service charge or the cost of new checks.

• Your total should match the balance listed on your bank statement.

• If it does not, find your mistakes, and make adjustments on your current stub.

• On rare occasions, the bank will make a mistake. If this happens, go to the bank with your checkbook and your statement, and work it out with them.

• If your total matches the balance on your bank statement, circle and check the verified — although possibly adjusted — balance in three places: on your stub, in your reconciliation, and on the bank statement.

• Save your cleared checks and your bank statement.

Final word:

• NEVER OVERDRAW YOUR ACCOUNT.

---

4. DEPOSIT ALL YOUR EARNINGS IN YOUR CHECKING ACCOUNT

Never cash a check made out to you. Deposit it in your bank account.

At the bottom of every deposit slip, there is a line labeled, "Less cash received." Never use this. It will confuse your records. The bank statement will show only the net amount deposited, and that won't match up with anything.

If you need cash, write a check for "cash" from your account and cash that.

This is the best way to keep your records accurate. You never know when you might want to review exactly what happened to your money. (You never know when the IRS might want to know exactly what happened to your money.)

5. PAY ALL YOUR BILLS WITH CHECKS

This is a must. It will give you proof you paid the bill. Use cash only for small purchases, or for things not tax deductible.

If you buy small items that are business expenses, you can pay cash, provided you keep the receipts and write on the receipt what it is for. When you get a few such receipts, total them, staple them together, and write a check for the full amount, payable to "cash." Write, "cash tags" on the check as your explanation. Put the number, amount, and date of the check on the stapled receipts. Keep a file of these cash tags. Go to the bank and cash the check to replace the money you spent out-of-pocket.

Now, when it comes time to figure out your income tax, you will have an accurate record and proof of your expenses, provided you . . .

6. . . . SAVE YOUR BANK STATEMENTS AND CHECKS

If you ever want to prove you paid something, the canceled check is the proof. This is especially true for the IRS. They insist on seeing the actual canceled checks in an audit where you are being asked to prove you spent the money the way your tax return says you did.

Never send a canceled check to anyone in the mail. Send a copy of both sides of the check, or a certified copy, if necessary. Always keep the original.

The IRS might also want to see your bank statements to verify your income (deposits).

How long should you keep these statements and checks? Some say three years, because it is thought that's as far back as the IRS audits you. This is not entirely true. They will ask for records from long ago to prove something that has been carried forward for years, like real estate "basis" or stock purchases.

NOTE: I realize my advice about checking accounts is a reflection of the way I do things, and is fairly dogmatic on several counts. It is a system developed over the years, and improved upon every time I learn how to avoid problems that come up. Some of the problems surface rarely in a lifetime, but if they can be prevented by a careful system, you might agree that it is worth the precaution.

I am hoping you won't have to make the same mistakes I have made or seen others make.

If you can develop a different system that works for you, without forgetting something important, that's fine, too.

7. PAY BILLS ON TIME OR EARLY

Paying bills on time builds good credit for the future, when you will want to get a loan to buy a house or finance a business. Paying bills late labels you as a poor risk and could prevent you from being approved for a loan. Even one or two late payments could make the difference, especially if your income is just barely enough to qualify for the loan.

Paying bills promptly also helps you develop a good working relationship with the people you rely on from time to time to help you run your business smoothly. People learn to trust you, and will give you good service when you need it.

I have always made it a practice to pay the plumbing service I use on the very day I receive the bill. When I have a plumbing problem in one of my rental units, they respond quickly. Why?

They know I value their time and the excellent quality of their work, because I always pay them promptly.

8. PAY "CASH" OR USE CREDIT CARDS AND PAY THEM OFF COMPLETELY EACH MONTH

Paying "cash" means not buying on time. It does not mean you don't write a check. Do write a check, or use a credit card.

If you have charge accounts, make sure you only charge what you can pay off each month. Never pay only the "minimum payment." THIS IS A TRAP, and many people fall into it.

If you carry a balance forward, interest is charged at a *very high rate,* plus interest can then be charged also on every new purchase you make the following month, even if you pay it off at the end of that month. Once you allow a "balance owed" to carry into the next month, a different set of rules is used. This is one of the most expensive ways to borrow money.

If you pay your bill completely each month, *no interest* is charged.

Charge accounts can be useful, but only if you are able to control your spending and pay off the accounts each month when the bill comes in the mail.

When shopping for a credit card, look for one with no annual "membership fee," and no finance charge when you pay the bill in full monthly. You won't care much what their finance charges are, if you are going to pay the entire balance each month.

9. LEARN ABOUT INCOME TAX

Have you heard about "Survival of the Fittest" in nature? The same thing applies when it comes to Income Tax. People who never bother to learn the tax laws or to live by them fall by the wayside on the road to success.

Already we have talked a lot about the Internal Revenue Service (IRS) and Income Tax. That's because almost everything you do is affected by some tax law.

In order to survive financially, you must learn as much as you can about income tax. What is taxable? What is not? What can be "deducted" from taxable income? Whenever you do anything

Learn about Income Tax

with money or possessions, you should think about the tax
rules, or you will be paying more taxes than you should.

Read the instruction booklet that comes with the Federal Tax
Forms. If you live in one of the many states that have State
Income Tax, you should become familiar with that, too.

Buy a good instruction book, such as *J. K. Lasser's Your
Income Tax.*

Practice filling out Schedule C for a business. At the very
least, you should *read* Schedule C to get an idea of what you will
be filling out at the end of the year. Tax forms are available at
banks, libraries, and Post Offices from the last week of
December to the first or second week of April, if the supply lasts.
You can get them any time at an IRS Office, or tax accountant's
office. The forms are free.

You will still probably want a professional tax accountant to
help you with your taxes. Have that person check what you have
already done and give you suggestions. They should know all
the latest changes in the law, and there usually are several each
year.

Last of all, FILE AN HONEST TAX RETURN. You'll sleep better, be more successful, and stay out of jail.

10. MAKE YOUR MONEY WORK FOR YOU

It's never too early to get acquainted with the Stock Market, Mutual Funds, Treasury Bills, or United States Government Bonds.

If your parents have a trusted family stock broker, you might speak to that person about your investment goals. Do you want to start an investment program that will help pay for college when you are ready? Travel to Europe when you graduate? Buy real estate? Start a business?

Your stock broker will make recommendations. One catch is the minimum amount required to get started. It could be $100, $500, or more for most mutual funds.

According to *Family Circle,* January 20, 1987 issue, there is at least one mutual fund (not available through stock brokers) that will let you open an account with a small amount of money. Twentieth Century Investors, Inc. in Kansas City, Missouri requires only $1 (or more) to get started. Read the book condensation of *How To Increase Your Net Worth,* by Paul N. Strassels and William B. Mead (probably available at your library).

11. SET GOALS

You've heard this before. Still, it is one of the most important things to do, if you want to succeed.

Dale Carnegie teaches goal setting. Louis Tice teaches it in his "New Age Thinking" course, and so does every other self-improvement teacher I know.

As you think of your financial, educational, or personal goals, be specific. Think about what, when, and perhaps even where. Don't worry about *how.* Your subconscious mind will figure that out for you. It works. You will see.

First, think of short-term goals and write each goal on a separate 3 x 5 card. For instance, "By the end of this year I will have $5,000 in my savings account." Or, "By the end of next

Reach . . .   . . . for your goal

semester, I will earn an extra $800 and buy the red Honda motorscooter at Scooter's, Inc."

Think about your goal and visualize yourself riding the red motorscooter. This is one of the most important things you must do to be successful, and it isn't work. It's fun!

Next, think of longer goals: five years, ten years, or more. Write them on cards. How about, "In eight years, by January 1, 1998, I will own a successful printing business in Palo Alto, California. I will have at least five employees, and the reception area will be clean and cozy. Customers will come in, sit down in a cushioned oak chair at a large round oak table, and look at sample letterheads and type-facing."

After you think of your goals and write them down, imagine yourself realizing your dream. Your subconscious will take over and point you toward your goals.

Think of your goals periodically. Read your cards occasionally.

You Deserve To Succeed

Now, do one more thing. Write on a 3 x 5 card, "I deserve to be happy and successful." Read this every day. It will help overcome negative feelings you might have about yourself.

Some people are not happy or successful because they feel they don't deserve such a good life. Success makes them feel guilty. If they are happy, somewhere someone else might be unhappy. If they make money, someone else must be losing money. Does this sound silly? It *is,* but it is also a very common problem, and we all think that way a little bit — at least, sometimes. We don't usually express it, because it doesn't make much sense. That doesn't stop us from thinking it, and thinking it is enough to have a bad effect on our success.

The way to fight this is to tell ourselves out loud every day, "I deserve to be happy and successful." Look into the mirror and say, "You deserve to be happy and successful." Tell each member of your family, "You deserve to be happy and successful." Tell your friends. Let them tell you. If you can't say, "I deserve to be happy and successful," out loud (because you are in a public place), think it in your mind. No matter where you are or what you are doing, you can say these words to yourself. In this way, you are programming your subconscious mind with positive thoughts, so it can more efficiently help you reach your goals.

12. LEARN TO HAVE FUN WITHOUT SPENDING MONEY

This applies to dates, too. There is no need to spend a lot of money every time you go out. You and your friends could probably think of at least fifty ways to have fun without spending money. I challenge you to try it.

1. That's the first way to have fun. Have a brainstorming session with your friends. Think of fifty ways to have fun without spending money.

2. Ride your bike, scooter, or skateboard.

Play ball . . .   Going . . .   Going . . .   Gone

Climb a tree—how's this for a fun date?

3. Go for a walk. Observe nature.

4. Look for four-leaf clovers in the lawn.

5. Jump rope alone or with friends. No matter how old you are, this is fun. The older you get, the more challenging it is.

6. Plant a garden with seeds harvested from flowers and vegetables gone to seed.

7. Play hopscotch (no matter how old you are).

8. Play tag, hide-and-seek, or "Sardines." Sardines is the reverse of hide-and-seek. One person hides, then everyone looks for him or her. As people find the hiding place, they crawl in, too, until they are packed like sardines. The first person to find the person hiding gets to be the one to hide next time.

9. Play touch-football or softball.

10. Visit the art gallery, museum, or aquarium.

11. Go to local historic attractions (sightseeing).

12. If you live in the country and have a horse, go horseback riding.

13. Go fishing. In California, if you are under sixteen, no license is required.

14. Attend free community events.

15. Participate in free school or church activities.

16. Look at old picture albums with family or friends.

17. Go to the library.

18. If transportation is not a problem, go to the airport and watch people.

19. Go to the park.

20. Play tennis.

21. Go swimming.

22. Watch the local college tennis team practice.

23. Watch college football practice.

24. Go for a walk around the local college campus.

25. Window shop after the stores are closed. Window shopping when the stores are open usually ends up costing money.

26. Visit the zoo.

27. Jog.

28. Go hiking.

29. Take a five or ten mile walk around the community. Have someone with a car help you map out a route, or use a city map and figure out the distance according to the scale on the map.

30. Organize a scavenger hunt.

31. Attend a city council meeting. Call the city to find out when they are held.

Visit local historic attractions   **Play tennis**

32. Attend a planning commission meeting.

33. Go to the courthouse and attend trials or hearings.

34. For a fun double date, park your car in the shopping mall parking lot after the stores are closed. Play dance music on the tape deck and dance in the empty parking lot. Try waltzing to Strauss.

35. On a clear, star-lit night, see how many constellations you can find. How many planets can you see? Watch for shooting stars.

36. Observe ants on the ground. Watch one ant for awhile. See where he goes and what his struggles are (especially if he is carrying something).

37. Write a story in a group. Everyone jumps in and carries the action along.

38. Read a story aloud to someone. Try some of Edgar Allan Poe's short stories.

39. Put on a play. Write and produce it.

40. START YOUR OWN BUSINESS. What could be more fun than that?

Caution: Don't underestimate the value of having fun without spending money. Observe. Look around. Watch kids in shopping malls and in video arcades. You will soon agree that most kids don't have much money because they spend it too fast on entertainment.

Avoid costly, harmful habits such as smoking, drinking, and drugs.

There is nothing to be gained and everything to be lost by acquiring any one of these habits. In addition to the obvious health hazards that have been well publicized, (plus other professional drawbacks discussed in Chapter 11), there is the further disadvantage of unnecessary cost.

Addictive habits make budgeting and saving much harder. People who smoke and/or drink and whose finances are always in a crisis mode sometimes do not have enough money to pay the rent, buy food, or buy shoes for their children — but they can and do buy cigarettes and beer (or other alcohol). Their compulsive habits dictate how they will spend their family's resources.

If you keep yourself from having to support an addictive habit, you will keep your freedom to choose how you will spend your money. The smoker gives up that freedom. The habitual alcohol or drug user gives up that freedom. "Ah," they say, "we can experiment with this, then quit." Wrong. You don't know — until too late — if you are genetically targeted to become addicted to alcohol or drugs after a very short period of use (possibly, even after the first time).

Sexual activity can also become addictive, and it is costly. There is an emotional price to pay, a physical price to pay, a spiritual price to pay, and a dollars and cents price to pay. Safe sex is expensive, and unsafe sex is even more expensive. Becoming a parent is a life-long commitment. It can be a wonderful experience when the time is right, or an unhappy one if the time is not right.

There are many risks: emotional risks and physical risks for both partners and for the potential child, spiritual risks, and financial risks.

My question is this: What are the benefits? I can't think of any. I can think of many compelling reasons kids have for becoming sexually active, but I can't think of any benefits. Maybe you can. If so, are the benefits worth the cost?

CHAPTER 3

BE A SURVIVOR

Some people seem to be born "survivors." They live with the quiet assurance that no matter what happens, they will make it.

You've heard of people who overcome every bad thing that gets in their way: accidents, illness, flood, famine, and earthquakes. Nothing conquers the spirit of a survivor. Living through hard times makes them stronger.

It might even look like there *are* no hard times for some survivors. They appear to be happy and successful without even trying.

What is a "survivor?"

A SURVIVOR:

• Enjoys working.

• Knows he can make it.

• Is creative. Comes up with new ideas and new ways to do things.

• Has the courage to act on his ideas.

• Can be objective.

• Gets excited about new projects.

• Knows that when something doesn't work, it is only a temporary set-back.

• Recognizes a good opportunity when he sees one.

- Listens to others, then decides for himself.
- Doesn't have to succeed at everything to be a success.

Are you doing some or all of these things now? Then you already know you are a survivor. If not, these are skills and attitudes you can learn. If survival is easy for some, it can still be learned by others.

Be a survivor.

Security is a strong, healthy body—excercise regularly

CHAPTER 4

SECURITY

Many people think security is working for a large company with a steady salary, lots of benefits, and a good retirement program.

What happens when the company changes ownership or management and fires you? What happens if the company has trouble because of a bad economy or because it loses large contracts, has to cut back the work force to make ends meet, and fires you?

Yesterday, I spoke to a man who is the vice-president of a large business. He has worked there for 27 years, but they are "letting him go," because they are being taken over by another corporation. In a few months, he will be out of work.

It's all right to have a job working for someone else, but it is a mistake to think it will last forever.

What is security?

SECURITY IS:

• Knowing you can make money on your own.

• Wanting to work and be productive.

• Having confidence in yourself as a survivor.

• The ability to spend wisely and save regularly.

• Having some good investments.

A strong, healthy body
Do everything you can to keep your good health

- Faith in God.

   Knowing we have a Heavenly Father who loves us and cares about our success is a wonderful source of strength.

- A good education, including a college degree.

   This might not get you a job, but it is an asset. Lack of education is usually a drawback.

- A strong, healthy body.

   A healthy body and physical strength are wonderful to have, and you will want to do everything you can to keep your good health. This should include staying away from drugs, alcohol, smoking, coffee, and sex outside of marriage. It should also include a balanced diet and regular exercise.

   Sometimes we lose our good health, anyway, because of illness or accident. Some people are born with physical handicaps. This does not mean loss of security, if we have some of the other things on this list.

- Good credit.

Learn to type

• A sense of humor.

• Liking people. Caring about others and treating them fairly.

• Good friends.

• Having the courage to make changes in your life.

• Being honest.

• Having many useful skills, such as:

  ▪ Being able to type.

  ▪ Knowing how to use a computer.

  ▪ Being able to drive a car and a small truck.

  ▪ Knowing how to use the telephone, the telephone directory, the yellow pages, a dictionary, a thesaurus, and a library.

  ▪ Sewing and cooking.

  ▪ Swimming, water safety, and First Aid.

Auto mechanics is a useful skill

- Music.

- Knowing how to add, subtract, multiply, divide, and use percentages.

- Artistic and creative ability.

- Speaking English correctly.

- Speaking and understanding a second language.

- Knowing how to write a letter, an article, a story, or a book.

- Being able to organize things so they are simple and make sense.

- Auto mechanics.

- Basic plumbing, electricity, telephone wiring, and home repair.

- Knowing how to use a hammer, saw, screwdriver, and drill.

- Being able to keep good records.

Learn how to swim

- Neat, legible handwriting .

- Knowing how to trim a tree, mow a lawn, plant a garden, paint a house, build a fire, and live outdoors.

- Having the ability to speak well to a group (public speaking).

- Basic courtesy and good table manners.

It is not necessary to have all the skills on this list, but it is good to have as many as possible.

You can learn a lot from your parents. If you are helping with chores around the house and yard, you will already have practice doing many of these things.

You can learn some skills in school and in after-school classes, clubs, or activities. The Cub Scout, Boy Scout and Girl Scout programs offer excellent opportunities to develop a variety of skills. Some, you can learn by working with or for someone who can teach you. The rest, you can teach yourself with how-to books, or by observing carefully and asking questions.

Learn how to . . .

. . .Trim a tree

. . . Play a musical instrument

PART TWO

SOME WAYS
TO MAKE MONEY

I hope you have as much fun picking out ways to make money as I have had thinking about them.

The first time you read through these ideas, mark those that interest you, so you can review them later.

A few of the projects suggested are not suitable for young children. For instance, in some cases a driver's license is needed, and sometimes, adequate physical size and strength are required.

For more detailed information on any of the activities mentioned in this section, go to your public library and look in the card catalog for books or other published material relating to the subject. Ask the librarian for help, if you can't find what you need.

Bring your own equipment and arrive prepared to work

CHAPTER 5

SERVICES

Know your business. Offer to perform a service only after you have experience and know what you are doing. Practice at home. Read books. Observe others.

Get whatever equipment the job requires, and learn how to take care of it. If you have your own equipment and arrive fully prepared to work, not only will it be easier to get jobs, but you can charge more.

People don't like to run around gathering up material you don't have or forgot to bring. That's usually the hardest part of the job, and if your customers have to get that involved, they will be sorry they hired you.

Cleaning up after yourself is very important. If your customers have to clean up after you, they will not feel like having you work for them again.

If you are mowing the lawn, don't step on the flowers. If you are sweeping the floor, don't bang up the baseboards or get the wall dirty. If you are washing windows, spread a drop-cloth inside to protect the walls and floors. Never track dirt into a house. Take off your shoes, if possible.

If you bring your own equipment, are careful not to damage anything, and remember to clean up after yourself, you won't have much competition, because very few workers observe these three rules. When I find someone who does, I remember to call them when I need another job done.

Practice at home

HERE ARE 78 WAYS TO MAKE MONEY THROUGH SERVICE

1. Baby Sitting

This is one of the oldest and most common ways for young people to make money. If you have younger brothers or sisters, you probably have some good experience. If not, there are usually classes offered in baby sitting at the community center or at school.

Child care is an important responsibility and should not be undertaken without experience or training.

Of course, baby sitting would not be an appropriate service for a young child to offer.

2. Teaching Children

There is a lot of emphasis these days on giving babies and young children opportunities to learn a variety of things. Mothers might appreciate some help with this very time-consuming project.

Go to the library and learn as much as you can about teaching babies and young children. See if you can develop some expertise in a few areas or methods of instruction. You might volunteer to help at a nursery school or kindergarten to gain some experience with children. Churches usually have nurseries and are always looking for help.

3. Tutoring

If you are good in one or several subjects, there are always other students who are not. Often, parents will hire tutors to help their children get better grades in subjects that are especially troublesome.

If you are good enough in these subjects, you can offer your services as a tutor.

This could be done through the school counseling program, ads on bulletin boards, ads in the school paper, or by talking to the teachers who teach those subjects you would like to tutor. Perhaps the teachers will refer you to parents of students who need help.

4. Entertaining At Children's Parties

Dress up like a clown, make animals out of balloons, perform magic tricks, lead the children in games, or tell jokes. This is one way to make money and have a lot of fun at the same time.

Some large companies hire people to entertain children of employees and guests at company functions or picnics.

5. Pet Walking

Many people are too busy to give their pets regular exercise. A pet walking service would be helpful to them and profitable for you.

6. Pet Sitting

There are two ways to offer this service. Take care of the pet in its own home by going there once or twice a day, or offer a "Pet Foster Home" service, and care for the pet in *your* home.

I recently heard of a service that offers a variety of "Foster Homes," each suited to different kinds of pets. Some people have large areas for larger animals, others have accommodations for smaller ones. Some homes prefer cats, others like dogs.

This is a new idea that appeals to pet owners, because it offers a loving home atmosphere for the pet, instead of the kennel environment. A pampered pet can receive the same careful attention at the foster home. If mealtime includes a special ritual, that ritual can be followed. If, at home, a dog gets sirloin steak for dinner, he can enjoy the same menu at the foster home. When pet owners return, they are greeted by a well-adjusted, happy pet, instead of a depressed, skinny animal that felt abandoned and refused to eat the whole time its owners were gone.

7. Pet Care

Bathing, grooming, and flea-dipping are troublesome chores for pet owners.

You could offer this service at your home, or theirs. You might pick-up and deliver as an extra convenience for your customers, if they prefer to have the bathing, etc. done away from their homes.

A warm welcome for guests at the pet foster home

Plus lots of love   =   A contented customer

8. Training Service for Pets

If you like animals and have some experience training your own, you could train pets (mostly dogs) for other people.

This might amount to taking the pet to obedience class for the owner.

Is it possible to house-break a pet for someone else? If you could figure out how to do that, you would be in great demand.

9. Cleaning Up After Pets

Many pet owners would welcome this type of weekly or twice-weekly service. In the case of several very large animals, like horses, a daily service might be necessary.

The fact that cleaning up after animals is not a pleasant task, should give you an endless supply of customers. It's the sort of thing pet owners don't like to do, but they know it has to be done.

You should be aware of potential health problems associated with animal feces. Dog, cat, and bird feces can harbor parasites that are harmful to humans. Call the County Health Department or the Department of Agriculture in your area. Go to the library and ask the Research Librarian to help you find out about this. The more you know, the better you can advertise your business, and the better you can protect yourself from these health hazards.

10. House Cleaning

Practice your house-cleaning skills at home. Read a good book on the subject. There are mistakes you do not have to make, such as using caustic cleaning products, and there are short cuts to learn that can save time and energy. A house properly cleaned will stay clean longer. Two good books on this subject are: *Clean Your House and Everything In It,* by Eugenia Chapman and Jill C. Major (Grosset & Dunlap) and *Speed Cleaning,* by Jeff Campbell.

11. Floor Sweeping, or Floor Care

If "House Cleaning" is too complicated for you, starting with specialty cleaning services might be a good idea.

Washing windows

The apprentice
"How am I doing?"

Floor sweeping is very specialized and easy to learn. You could branch out into simple mopping, scrubbing and waxing, or care of hardwood floors.

12. Window Washing

Another specialty is washing windows. It is not just a matter of getting the window wet, then wiping it dry. There are many things to be learned that will save time and produce a professional result. Read the chapter on windows in *Clean Your House & Everything In It*. If you don't have access to that book, go to the library and find other books or magazines with tips on window washing. If you can do a good job at a reasonable price, you will have a lot of steady customers for this service.

13. Washing and Ironing Clothes

You could either pick up and deliver, or do the laundry in your customer's own home.

Mothers of young children might want this kind of help, so they can spend more time with their children. Working mothers would be excellent candidates for this service.

In your advertising, point out to mothers the benefits of being relieved of household chores and spending more quality time with their children.

14. Yard Care

Mowing lawns, watering, weeding, and sweeping walks are services included in the category of yard care.

If you plan to offer weeding, make sure you know the difference between a weed and a non-weed.

There is a new weeding gadget on the market that actually works. It is simply a three-foot wooden pole with two short, barbed prongs attached to one end. To use it, you jab the prongs into the dirt on either side of the plant, and twist. You can easily uproot most plants that spring up in the lawn, like thistles and dandelions — tap root and all. The best part is that you don't even have to bend over.

Caution: Avoid chemical weed killers. Researchers are still trying to find out which ones are harmful to humans and to nature.

You should have your own power mower for mowing lawns.

Be sure to inquire about sprinklers. Notice their location. If they are the pop-up variety, sometimes they do not pop back down. Check before you begin mowing. You don't want to break a sprinkler, and you don't want to break the lawn mower. You can be sure you won't keep your job long, if you shear off sprinkler heads. If it does happen, repair them or have them repaired (if you don't know how).

15. Feeding Plants and Fertilizing Lawns

Home owners generally have a hard time knowing how and when to feed and fertilize. Many professional gardeners do not concern themselves with this important aspect of plant care.

Watch out for sprinklers

There is a good opportunity here for someone to step in and offer this specialized service. Of course, you must know what you are doing. If you could take a class on the subject of plant food and fertilizer, that would be good. Otherwise, read gardening books and talk to nursery store workers where plant food is sold. Find out what to use and how often to use it. Follow directions on the packages.

Roses, azaleas, rhododendrons, gardenias, fruit trees, and citrus trees are examples of plants that do better if they are properly fed. Learn what plants or trees in your area require regular feeding. Notice yards that have some of these plants. You might begin by offering your service to those yard owners.

16. Pruning

Depending on where you live, this could be another service in great demand. Plants grow, and certain ones should be pruned regularly. If they are not, they can become unattractive and might even have to be removed. Plants that are grafted to heartier root stock, like some fruit trees, nut trees, and roses, will be taken over by shoots from the stem below the graft, if they are not properly trimmed. Fruit trees might break under the burden of their own fruit, if they have not been pruned correctly.

Take a class in pruning, read books, watch and learn from an expert. If you get good at this, you will have a valuable skill.

Buy some good pruning shears. I paid $25.00 for a pair of gear-driven shears with aluminum handles. They are easy to operate and have lasted for years. The cheaper types are hard to use and break easily.

Don't try to work on large trees, since it can be dangerous and requires special training, as well as an experienced ground crew. If you enjoy climbing trees, and if you are strong enough and old enough, you might decide to learn this trade by working for a reputable tree care service.

17. Picking Pests

Some plant pests are best eliminated by picking them off the plants one-by-one.

When I was about six years old, living in Alexandria, Virginia, we had our first Japanese Beetle invasion. For several summers, these beautiful but destructive beetles clustered on bushes and plants and stripped them of everything green. The only defense at that time was to pick them off by hand. Our parents paid us a few cents per hundred. My brother and I went around with jars of water and picked Japanese Beetles. When the Department of Agriculture came up with a permanent cure, we were out of work.

Snails are a problem where I live now. See Chapter 7: Getting Paid Twice, for a discussion of snails.

18. Picking Produce

Sometimes people work hard to get a garden started, but when the plants mature, they realize they planted too much, or they just don't have time to pick the produce regularly. Maybe they go on vacation and need a picking service.

The reason picking is important is because plants will keep bearing longer, if ripe fruit and vegetables are not left on the plant. Strawberries are very time-consuming to pick. So are beans, peas, and cherry tomatoes.

You can offer to pick for a fee and give all your pickings to the garden owner, or you could take produce as pay, or a combination of both. See Chapter 7: Getting Paid Twice.

19. Rototilling

If you are old enough and strong enough, this is a profitable business.

First, you must have access to or own a rototiller. Perhaps you could borrow money from your parents to buy one. You could pay them 20% of the money you make until you have paid off the loan. You will probably want to rent one at first, to see if this is what you really want to do.

You will also have to find a way to transport the rototiller to the job. A small pick-up truck would be nice. If you have one, that's fine. If you have a friend with a truck, maybe you could be partners.

This is a seasonal business. There is not much call for it in the winter, but if you keep track of your customers, you could have repeat business every year in the Spring and Summer.

Many newspapers have a special section in the classified ads for services. This is a good place to advertise rototilling.

20. Cleaning Rain Gutters and Down-Spouts

A hose to flush out the down-spouts, a bucket for debris, an extension ladder, and a truck to haul the ladder are necessary in the gutter-cleaning business. If you stick to single-story houses, you could use a smaller ladder and might not need a truck.

This is a dirty job, and most homeowners would gladly pay to have someone else do it.

If you keep good records, it should be easy to go back twice a year, year after year. If you contact your customers before the first rains in the Fall, they usually will not have thought yet about cleaning their gutters, but will be glad to have you do it, when you remind them.

It is important to clean up after this job, or to keep from making a mess in the first place.

21. Hauling Debris

This is another good business, if you have a truck.

Shop around for the least expensive dump site. Dumps are usually cheaper for residents than non-residents, so begin looking in your own city or county.

22. Drip Systems

Watering plants and vegetable gardens with a drip system is usually more efficient than most other methods.

Installing a drip system is like playing with Tinker-Toys. It's fun, and it's easy, once you learn how. Practice on your own garden. Go to your local sprinkler system supply house and see what things are available. Get an instruction booklet and catalogue.

23. Sprinkler Systems

While you are looking into drip systems, look at regular sprinkler systems. This can also be fun, except it usually involves digging trenches.

24. Shoveling Snow

If you live in a climate where it snows, this is a good way to earn money in the wintertime. Convert your rototiller to a snowplow, and tackle some of the bigger jobs.

25. Vacation Watering Service

Water lawns, plants, and gardens for people when they go out of town.

26. Complete Vacation Service

Come to the property every day and pick up any newspapers left by mistake or on purpose. Pick up circulars, mail, notes, or anything else the residents would pick up, if they were home.

We came back from vacation once to find our driveway full of newspapers thrown there as complimentary copies by a paper to which we did not subscribe.

Detailing

Car washing

The complete vacation service might also include watering the lawn or checking the sprinkler system, if there is one, adding water to the pool, watering house plants, and possibly, feeding pets.

27. Car Washing, Waxing, and Detailing

You could offer this service at their house or at yours.

"Detailing" a car goes beyond mere washing and waxing. It involves thoroughly cleaning and polishing everything in and on the car. It takes several hours, and should leave the car looking like new, if possible. If you are good at this, you will get referrals and repeat business.

28. Car Washing for Dealers

Cars displayed in new or used car lots get dirty, just sitting there. You could speak to several car dealers about hiring you to keep their cars looking nice on the outside. It should be less expensive for them to have you do this, than to have one of their employees do it.

29. Lawn and Plant Care for Stores

Some stores have small lawns or a few flowers in window boxes. It doesn't take much work to keep a small lawn or a few flowers looking nice, if it is done regularly. The store manager or owner might be very happy to have your reliable service relieve him of this task.

30. Indoor Plant Service

There are lots of people who would like to have nice house plants, but end up killing off every plant they get. Such a person might welcome an indoor plant service.

You could provide the plants and care for them weekly, or they could buy the plants, and you could take care of them.

Of course, you must have a "way" with plants and be able to make them flourish. Proper watering and light are important. Feeding, re-potting, and pruning must be done correctly, and choosing the right plant for a given location makes things easier for everyone.

If you like house plants, you might already have an inventory of nice ones you have grown from cuttings. An indoor plant service gives you a built-in market for your plants.

31. Services for The Elderly

If you enjoy older people, you could offer services such as shopping, driving them to the store or anywhere else they want to go, reading to them, going for walks, playing chess, visiting daily or weekly, or calling to remind them what day it is.

Families of the elderly person living alone would appreciate having someone to help with these basic needs.

32. Helping Someone Else Run A Garage Sale

Holding your own garage sale is discussed in Chapters 6 and 7. Helping someone else is a service, and is therefore briefly mentioned here.

33. Caddying

Jan Leasure's book, *Big Bucks for Kids,* has a good description of Caddying beginning on page 28. To get a job, you first meet

"Hey, Mister, I think you should have used your 5-iron"

Once you have your route, you're in business

the Caddie Master, fill out an application, and take a small written test.

If you know how to play golf and enjoy the game, you might also enjoy caddying.

34. Delivering Newspapers

The paper route is a very traditional way for young people to make money. There might be a waiting list for just the right route close to home, but once you have your paper route, you are in business.

If you deliver your papers as early as you can every day, are careful to leave the paper where the subscriber wants it, and wrap the paper on rainy days, you will have nothing but satisfied customers.

35. Painting House Numbers

Call the city and see if you can get a permit to paint house numbers on the curb. Find out if they require a specific kind of paint and a certain style for the numbers. Buy a stencil of the right size and style, so the numbers will be uniform.

You will have to ask each home owner if they would like your service, and if they will pay you for it. The city might give you a permit, but they probably won't be interested in paying you to do the work. That does not mean you shouldn't ask the city if they will hire you. They might surprise both of us and say, "Yes."

36. Want Ads

Check the Want Ad section of your local newspaper from time to time. You might find someone who needs a job done that's right up your alley.

37. Pet Placement Service

Finding homes for kittens and puppies is a fun job. You could do this in various ways.

I have found it most efficient to take the puppies or kittens to a shopping center. If you are giving them away, you can usually get permission to do this. It took me twenty minutes per pet to find good homes in this way. I have also taken one or two puppies to a movie theater, where people are standing in line or just coming out of the movie. You meet hundreds of people in a few minutes and can usually find someone who wants a puppy or kitten.

Write down the names and addresses of each person who takes a pet. The owner might wish to follow up to be sure their pets have indeed found good homes.

38. Party Service

Offering to act as waiter or waitress for someone having a party could be fun. You might team up with your friends for large parties, and your service could include cleaning up.

39. Catering

You could go one step further and actually provide the food for a party, as well as serve it. If you enjoy parties and making fancy food, you might be very good at this.

... Only two left

Pet placement
service

40. Party Planning

If you really like parties and entertaining, you might want to
offer a service that would include planning the party and carrying out the plan. As you gain experience, you might decide to
plan weddings, receptions, and other large functions.

41. Organizing Competitive Events

First, check with your local city government to see if they have
any regulations about this activity. If their rules make it impossible for you to make any money at this, you will have to do it for
fun, for charity, or not at all.

Some possible events would be foot races, a marathon, a
swimming meet, a croquet tournament, horseshoe tournament,
tennis match, or any other event you personally enjoy and
understand and have the facilities to hold. That is, if you are
planning a swimming event, you must have access to a suitable
pool, etc.

42. Servicing Med-Fly Traps

Visit the Department of Agriculture locally, and see if they will pay you to service their Med-fly traps (or other bug traps, if you do not live in a Med-fly area).

43. Mail Service

Businesses can arrange with the Post Office to have someone pick up their mail early in the morning. This would be an advantage to many people, if they didn't have to pick it up themselves.

Most small businesses probably don't even know about this possible convenience. Early mail could be very important to tax accountants, especially in March and April. Title Companies and Real Estate Companies might benefit from this service.

Once you find someone who wants you to pick up and deliver their mail, have them fill out a form available from the Post Office, identifying you as their designated representative. Your fee for this would depend on the amount of mail you would be picking up, how often (once or twice a day,) how far away the customer is from the Post Office, and whether they want you to carry mail back to the Post Office.

The Post Office charges for making the mail available, but you can either have your customer pay the Post Office directly, or you can pay them and add the cost to your fee.

44. Stuffing, Sealing, and Stamping

People who do bulk mailing or mail order soliciting need help stuffing, sealing, and stamping envelopes. If their operation includes orders coming in, they will also need help opening the mail.

Someone who runs this type of business out of their home is probably looking for a good worker like you. Ask around. It won't take you long to find such an opportunity.

45. Formaldehyde Testing

Formaldehyde gas is a recently discovered form of indoor air pollution. It escapes from certain types of insulation, and manufactured wood held together by certain kinds of glue. Particleboard is a common offender.

There is a testing machine on the market which is supposed to measure the level of formaldehyde gas in the air. If you had the machine, you could offer a formaldehyde testing service. Look in your telephone book in the Yellow Pages under, "Air Pollution Measuring Equipment."

46. Painting Houses and Fences

If you have some experience, the right equipment, and a knack for it, you can do very well in this business.

People who own rental houses and apartments are always looking for good painters who are reasonably priced and who can do a job quickly, when it needs to be done. Houses or apartments that stand vacant, waiting to be painted, are losing money.

You should be able to paint the inside of a one-bedroom apartment in one or two days, depending on whether you do the woodwork, and whether you put on a second coat. If one coat does not cover well, by all means, apply a second coat. The second coat of paint goes on surprisingly fast and makes a huge difference in the final appearance of your work.

Painting the outside of a house is fairly easy, after you do the proper preparation. Working with a friend is more fun and makes the work go faster. Two people should be able to paint the outside of a small, two-bedroom stucco house in about three days.

Always be sure you have the right kind of paint and the right brushes or rollers for the job. The wrong material or equipment makes the work much harder. Remember, when you sell your services, you are selling time. Give yourself a break and your customer good value by using equipment and material that will save both time and energy.

When painting wooden houses or fences, be sure you know what kind of wood you are painting. Some kinds of wood, such as redwood, require special types of stain, as opposed to paint.

47. Reminder Service

This is a fun idea with many possibilities. All you need is a customer and a good filing system. For every day of the year, you

Make sure you have
the right brush
for the job

have a space for entries. You don't need a computer, though it would be useful.

Some people have trouble remembering birthdays, anniversaries, and other special events. This often causes lots of embarrassment. You could offer to remind them of these dates two weeks in advance, then one week, then one day before.

You could also offer to provide a selection of cards, or help them even more by shopping for an appropriate gift.

48. Card Service

Send seasonal greeting cards to clients for businesses or salespeople.

You could either get your cards wholesale, or produce your own.

49. Distributing Samples or Leaflets

If you can find customers, this seems like a good job for most any age. You simply walk from house to house and leave off samples, leaflets, or phone books. Phone books are heavy, and would be more difficult. For leaflets, you could use your bike, walk with a shoulder bag, or pull a wagon.

> *Caution:* Never place anything inside the mailbox. This is illegal, and you could be subject to a fine. Also, the mailman might come along behind you and gather up everything you have distributed.

50. Talent Clearing House

Find out what your friends can do, what skills or experience they have, and set up a clearing house for this talent. You can then offer a variety of services.

You could charge a percentage of what your workers make, or you could charge them a flat referral fee.

51. Limousine Service

In order to offer this service, you will have to be at least 18 years old. A special license might be required in your state, in addition to a regular driving permit or license. You will need a car and adequate insurance.

Your main source of customers would be people who need a ride to or from the airport.

52. Cleaning Fireplaces

Sometimes fireplaces go unused, because getting the fireplace dirty means taking out ashes.

You could offer a weekly service to clean the fireplace and dispose of the ashes. (You might even find a market for the ashes as fertilizer, or a component of fertilizer.)

Cleaning the chimney is another, more complicated matter. You could do that, too, if you have the training.

The main challenge you will have when cleaning fireplaces or chimneys is preventing the fine ash-dust from puffing up and flying out into the room. Sometimes, spraying a mist of water over the ashes helps. If you have a partner, one person could hold a vacuum cleaner hose above the work area and vacuum any dust right out of the air.

53. Delivery Service

A car would be nice, but a bike will do, if your delivery area isn't spread out too far.

You could deliver letters, packages, flowers, telegrams, groceries, or prescriptions for a drug store.

54. Delivery Service for Garage Sales

If you have a truck, you could contact people who are advertising garage sales and see if they need help delivering larger items. You could work for the seller or the buyer.

If you can't contact them before the sale, ride around to all the sales being held and offer your service.

55. Fashion Show

Perhaps a local children's clothing store would pay you to organize a fashion show, featuring their fashions. Something like this might be more successful if you were to contribute part of the proceeds to a charity or cause, like new playground equipment.

56. Bicycle Repair

If you are good at repairing your own bicycle, you could get paid to repair bikes for others.

57. Automobile Repair

Someone who is really into automobile mechanics could be good at fixing or servicing cars for friends, teachers, parents, and other referrals.

58. Publicity, or Advertising Service

You could promote events or advertise things for sale with posters, bulletins, fliers, and notices on bulletin boards. Write news releases, or short public relations articles about your client's activity, and send them to the local newspapers.

Automobile repair service

If you had your own neighborhood newspaper, you could promote events and advertise things in it. The neighborhood newspaper is in Chapter 6: Things To Sell.

Taking down the posters and bulletins would be part of your service.

59. Thesaurus Hotline

If you're good with words and writing, you could provide a service for anyone looking for just the right word. Besides the well known *Roget's Thesaurus,* there are other reference books, such as *The Synonym Finder,* by J. I. Rodale, published by Rodale Press.

One way to charge your clients would be by the word, and collect monthly, when you have a sizeable bill.

60. Research Service

Professional writers often need help doing research for books, articles, or stories they are writing. If you enjoy doing research, this might be the business for you.

61. Marketing Service for Writers

There are many good writers who write excellent, saleable material, but never try to find a market for their work. Either they don't know how, or they are afraid of rejection. You can find these people in writing classes and writers' groups.

Once you learn the ropes, it is a matter of knowing the markets, submitting, rewriting, and submitting again and again. Writers are often very poor business people. That's where you can help, by offering to market their material for them.

62. Protest or Social Reform

Sometimes people have wonderful causes they would like to pursue, but don't ever get around to it because they haven't the time or don't know how.

You could offer a service to agitate for someone else's cause. Write letters to "The Editor" of your local newspaper, to state or U.S. Senators and Representatives, or to whomever the issue requires. Make phone calls. Gather signatures on a petition (unless the petition involves a ballot proposal, and you have to be a registered voter to get signatures). Send the petition to members of congress and to the newspapers.

Of course, it would be best to accept only causes you feel are worthwhile.

63. Practical Joke Service

If you enjoy practical jokes, you could make a business out of it. However, this is one type of business where you would have to be extra careful to make sure that what you do is not harmful in any way. You would not want to destroy property or damage anyone's reputation.

There are a lot of fun ways to play good, clean jokes on people, and if you are talented at this, you are already thinking of several funny, but harmless things you could do.

64. Moving Service

This is another business for someone with a driver's license and a truck.

It would be good to have a friend join in this venture with you, as it takes two people to lift some things.

If you decide to do this, you should know the best ways to lift and carry without hurting yourself. You could use a "dolly" for heavy boxes and large items, and hopefully, you would not attempt to move anything that is much too heavy or awkward for you.

65. Manual Labor

One way to make money and develop muscles at the same time is to do manual labor. There is always a demand for someone who can do hard work, such as digging holes or ditches, hauling dirt, carrying bricks, stacking wood, or moving furniture.

66. Dirty Work

"You name it, and if it isn't illegal, immoral, or too dangerous, we'll do it." This could be your slogan. You could crawl under the house, rescue cats from trees, scrub lawn furniture, or wash walls.

67. Knife and Scissors Sharpening

This seems to be a disappearing art. If you have the equipment and the know-how, a sharpening service would be a big help to a lot of people.

68. Typing

There is always work for good typists. If you have access to a word processor, that would be even better. You could offer to type papers, manuscripts, or theses for graduate students.

69. Computer Games

If you are good with computers, you might be able to write new programs or develop new games and sell them to software companies.

Computer-Tutor

70. Computer Consulting

People who are trying to learn how to use computers or word processors often feel they need special instruction. You could offer a consulting service to help others master a new computer, a new program, or a word processor.

71. Shoe Shine Business

Is this a vanishing service, or is it my imagination? These days, a good pair of shoes costs a lot of money. One way to make shoes last longer is to protect them with polish and waterproofing. People don't seem to be wearing overshoes as much as they used to, so a good shine is even more important now.

A homemade shoe-shine box and some polish, brushes, and rags are all you need to get started. Of course, you must know how to shine shoes and which products to put on different types of shoes. Some good spray-on waterproofing products are available and work quite well.

72. Organizing

Working and living in a messy, unorganized way is tiring and unproductive. Unfortunately, most of us slip into poor work habits or a haphazard life style and continue that way until guilt or necessity forces us into some attempt at reform. All too often, our efforts to "get organized" fail, because we lack the skill to think of a better system and to make it work.

If you are blessed with the gift of efficiency, or if you have studied and mastered the art of organizing, you can teach others. Show people how to arrange their kitchens, offices, closets, drawers, garages, or workbenches. Teach time management. Work with people in their own homes or give lectures.

73. Assembly Service

Many things we order through the mail or buy in stores come with "some assembly required." Upon opening the package, we are faced with a project that could take one hour for a simple stool, two or three hours for a lawn mower, ping-pong table, or tricycle, five hours for a garden cart, or two days for a piece of exercise equipment.

Most people have a hard time successfully completing complicated projects,and would gladly pay someone to do it. If you are mechanically inclined, you can offer an assembly service.

74. Installation Service

After buying our first video cassette recorder, my husband and I couldn't wait to get home and "hook it up." Never in our wildest dreams could we have foreseen the frustrating process this "simple" installation turned out to be. The instruction manual was translated from some foreign tongue and had omitted a few very pertinent facts.

For a novice, when it comes to newfangled devices, the complications are endless, and acquisition of the latest equipment can be a terrible mistake—unless there is a talented young person who can help with the installation for a reasonable fee.

If you are skilled in this field, offer an installation service for TV's, VCR's, Hi-Fi equipment, CD players, and other electronic paraphernalia.

75. Lifeguard Service

If you are a strong, capable swimmer, enjoy swimming, and are 15 or over, call a local chapter of the American Red Cross, and find out when they are offering their next "Lifesaving: Rescue and Water Safety Class." After you have taken the class and passed a final test, you will receive a certificate, which qualifies you to be a lifeguard.

With this certification, you can offer your services as a free-lance lifeguard for private pool parties, or you could work at a public pool or private swimming club. When several people are using a swimming pool, there is the possibility of someone having an accident or wandering into deep water, when they can't swim.

In the case of a diving accident, it is important to have a trained person present to direct the lifesaving effort. If correct precautions are taken, further injury to the neck and spinal chord (which could lead to paralysis) can be prevented. This is one of the many procedures you will learn and practice in your Lifesaving Class.

Being a lifeguard is a serious responsibility, and adequate liability insurance coverage is important.

76. Repair Service

Repairing small appliances or other devices with moving parts is easy for people who are mechanically inclined. If you are such a person, you could help people save money by repairing things for them at less than replacement cost.

77. Helping Invalids

People who do not have the use of their arms or legs need help to perform simple, everyday actions. Often their minds are alert, but their bodies are helpless. Caring for the bedridden is very time-consuming and difficult for family members— especially when the condition is permanent.

If you have a lot of patience, or enjoy serving others and are willing to learn how to perform tedious, repetitious tasks for someone else, you will earn rewards far beyond any money you receive in this type of service.

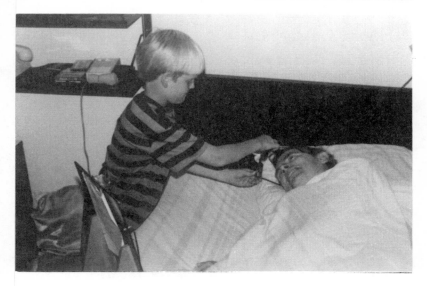

Is this OK?

No matter how young you are, you can help people who cannot help themselves, by adjusting their glasses, then turning the pages of a book, while they read or study. You can write letters or papers for them, if they are taking courses, or simply visit and keep them informed of things happening in their neighborhood or community.

It is a wonderful feeling to know someone is looking forward to your arrival and the time you spend with them.

78. Black and White Film Processing

Commercial film processing services presently cater to color-film users. You can get a roll of color film developed and printed in one hour, but a roll of black and white film takes a week.

A few years ago, black and white film was used more than color. Color film and color processing were expensive and slow.

Now, black and white picture taking is practically obsolete—except for newspapers, books, or other mass reproductions. Because the market is limited, there is no reasonable service available for processing black and white film.

If your hobby is photography, and you have a darkroom set up in your basement or spare bathroom, you could offer a 1-day developing and printing service for black and white pictures.

Contact local film processing services—especially those that offer 1-hour or 1-day service for color film. Offer to work as their sub-agent, so they will have a way to offer faster service for black and white film, as well.

CHAPTER 6

THINGS TO SELL

Before selling anything, find out what permits are required, and whether or not you should be collecting a sales tax. Look in the phone book under, *"State:* Taxes." Call and find out what the rules are for your state.

OVER 100 THINGS TO SELL

1. Life Story

Write a person's life story, and sell copies to that person or their family. Elderly people might enjoy having their histories written and made available to their children, grandchildren, and great-grandchildren. They might want to give copies to family members for Christmas.

2. Jokes

Collect jokes; compile and index them according to subject. People who give speeches are always looking for good stories to tell. Also, people like to read jokes just for fun.

3. Bargain Directory

Read the weekly ads from the newspaper and direct mailings. Compile an alphabetical directory for different items, and the prices at different stores. You could have a section for groceries, and one for appliances, hardware, gardening supplies, etc.

Recycling

Regular subscribers to your service would know at a glance where to go for the best price. They should be happy to pay for your directory, as it will save them much more.

4. Recycling

Newspapers, aluminum cans, regular cans, and bottles are garbage to the ordinary household.

You can collect these things and sell them to recycling centers, junkyards, or manufacturers. Safeway Grocery Stores buy aluminum cans in our area.

Of course, if bottles have deposits, you can return them to stores where they are sold and collect the deposit.

5. Carpet Scraps

When new carpeting is installed, there are always scraps of different sizes left over. Ask the carpet stores or installers if you can have pieces they would otherwise throw away. If you know someone who is having carpeting installed, ask them.

You could use the scraps to make area rugs, or you might have enough for car floors.

6. Signs

Make or have made signs that say, "Allergy, No Smoking, Please." The kind you can stick to any surface are very useful for non-smokers.

You can order these from a sign-printing company. Look in the Yellow Pages. Compare prices. If you order a large number, they cost less per sign.

Other signs would sell, too, but I know there is a demand for this one.

7. Amway

If you are 16 or over, and your parents give their permission, you can sell Amway products.

8. Tupperware

Tupperware has no age limitation, though it is best to have your parents' permission and support.

9. Birdhouses

There are lots of simple, yet clever ways to build birdhouses or bird feeders, and what could be more fun? Design your own. It would be interesting to make one with a see-through wall, so you could watch the birds through the window.

Birdhouses and feeders are surprisingly expensive, if you try to buy them, considering the small amount of material involved and the ease with which they can be built.

10. Baskets

If you could learn how to weave different kinds of baskets, you could make them from material found in nature, just as native basket-weavers do. You could even use magazine pages, or left-over wallpaper. If your material doesn't cost you anything, you could make a good profit.

Baskets are popular items, and bring a nice price, if they are well done.

11. House Numbers

Hand-crafted wooden house numbers are not easy to find. You could develop your own style and make them to order.

12. Planter Boxes

You might be able to make planter boxes out of scraps from the lumberyard, but they should be made from a weather-resistant type of material, such as redwood, unless you plan to line them or paint them.

13. Gingerbread Houses

These sell very readily during the Christmas season, but could also sell at other times of the year.

I know two girls who made Gingerbread Houses to order, for real estate agents who gave them to their clients on special occasions.

14. Golf Balls

You can gather used golf balls along the perimeter of a golf course, or you could ask for permission to "shag" or hunt balls on the golf course early in the morning or late at night.

After you clean and sort the balls, you can sell them back to the golfers.

15. Worms

If you live in an area where there are a lot of people who enjoy fishing, you could either raise worms or gather them.

It is fun to hunt for "night-crawlers" in the lawn after dark. Night-crawlers are large earthworms that come out of the ground at night. If you are very quick, you can catch them. It is best to have someone hold the flashlight while you dive for the worms, or vice versa.

Worms for sale
"How about these beauties?"

16. Seedlings

Every year there are hundreds of "volunteer" seedlings that
come up in the garden, in the flower beds or in the lawn. These
same types of plants are sold in nurseries.

In our yard we have young loquat trees, eucalyptus trees, oak
and walnut trees, plum trees, redwood trees, nectarine trees,
peach trees, and apple trees coming up from seeds. Fruit trees
might not bear good fruit if grown from seeds, but they are still
nice plants.

In addition to volunteers, you can easily start plants from
seeds flowers produce when they finish blooming and "go to
seed." Marigolds, poppies, sunflowers, and many other varieties
produce lots of seeds you can easily gather.

17. Plants from Clippings or Roots

Many plants multiply by sending out runners or roots, such
as blackberries, strawberries, ivy, mint, bamboo, or equisetum.

In fact, blackberries, ivy, and mint spread so quickly that they will take over a garden in no time and become almost impossible to control. I have had this unpleasant experience. These plants are best grown in a confined area, such as a planter box or in a space surrounded by cement walks or an asphalt driveway.

Other plants can be started by trimming the plant and poking the cuttings into dirt. In Virginia, we used to start forsythia this way. In California, geraniums grow readily, and clippings are almost guaranteed to thrive. Coleus and many other house plants can be grown from cuttings.

Succulents such as Christmas Cactus, African Violets, or "Hen and Her Chickens" can be started from a leaf.

18. Vegetable Plants

Tomatoes, squash, cucumbers, peas, and beans are examples of vegetables you can start indoors several weeks before the planting season. It is not difficult, if you have the space and a warm location.

Most people don't start thinking about their garden until it is time to set the plants out. Then they go to the store and buy their vegetables already started, instead of using seeds. Every Spring there is a good market for these plants.

19. Vegetables

Grow your own vegetable garden and sell your produce to local stores or directly to people in your neighborhood. You might be able to set up a stand in front of your house. (Check with the city.)

Health food stores are particularly interested in produce grown without chemical fertilizers or toxic sprays.

20. Flowers

Grow flowers in your garden. You could sell cut flowers or flower arrangements. After you get established, you could do arrangements to order.

Grow vegetables
and flowers

21. Bonsai

"Bonsai" is a Japanese term for the art of growing carefully trained dwarfed plants. If you learn how to do this, you will be able to create beautiful plants to sell.

22. Herbs

Growing herbs is a whole subject in itself. Learning about the different herbs and their uses would be interesting and helpful.

23. Dried Flowers and Weeds

You can gather dried flowers and weeds from your garden, from meadows and fields, or beside the road. They can be sold in arrangements or in bunches.

24. Dried Herbs

Dried herbs, ready for cooking, can be packaged and sold. You will, of course, harvest them from your own herb garden.

25. Sachets

Dried herbs and/or dried flower petals can be made into attractive, sweet-smelling sachets.

26. Balloons

You could sell balloons filled with gas, or balloons made into animals, or balloons on strings or sticks. The metallic balloons are a potential hazard. When they escape into the air, they often become tangled in power lines and can cause expensive damage. Don't sell them. Power companies have announced their intention to fix liability and recover losses, when possible.

27. Cookbook

How about a neighborhood cookbook? Gather recipes from people in your area and compile them into a cookbook.

If you have a computer with a word processor and printing capabilities, you could print your own. Or, if you have a copy machine, you could reproduce your book that way.

Otherwise, you will shop around for printers or other copying services.

28. Calendars

Make your own calendars and sell them. They could appeal to a particular group of people by including certain pictures or sayings.

29. Candles

Make and sell candles. They could be scented, fancy, or plain.

30. Family Pictures or Video Tapes

Take pictures of children, pets, families, family functions or activities, such as Little League. Sell the pictures to the family or families involved.

You could take a chance, or take orders.

Take pictures of pets
Photo by Philip R. Monson, age 14

31. Small Business Directory

People will pay to be listed in your small business directory, which is to be distributed throughout the community.

A project like this one, or the neighborhood cookbook, might be more successful if you pledge some percentage of your proceeds to a worthy cause in your community.

32. Ad Book

This is along the same lines as the small business directory, except it would *not* be in the form of a directory, and it would include ads from any business or service that wished to participate.

The book could be just ads, or it could include some articles or handy tips, or pictures of people, places, or events in your community.

Again, you might be able to sell more ads, if you agree to give some of your profits to a local cause.

33. Seeds

Harvest flower and vegetable seeds from plants that are not hybrids. (Sometimes hybrids will not produce good seeds.) Package and sell the seeds.

34. Berries

If you live in certain parts of the country, you can pick wild blackberries, blueberries, or elderberries and sell them.

You don't have to worry about growing the plants, since they are wild. But you will need to watch out for poison ivy, poison oak, and ticks. You can't see ticks ahead of time, but you can remove them from your scalp and skin easily, if you find them right away. My mother used to look through my hair for ticks before I went to bed at night, if I had been out picking berries.

35. Fruit

If you have fruit trees or citrus trees on your property, you will probably have more fruit than you can use at one time. Sell it.

36. Paper Logs

There is a gadget on the market called a "log rolling machine" that enables you to roll newspapers into paper logs. With a little practice, you can produce good "logs," which you can then sell.

37. Firewood

Gather firewood and sell it. A truck would be helpful for this. You can get permission or a permit, if necessary, to pick up dead wood from forested areas, or you can contact professional tree care services to see if they have wood you can haul away for them. Often, they have large branches or logs that need to be split and that no one wants because of the work involved.

Wood that has had a chance to dry out usually sells better than freshly cut "green" wood, and brings a higher price.

Real juice 25¢
Service with a smile

38. Popsicles

You can develop your own recipe for tasty popsicles. If your mother uses canned fruit, you could use the extra juice in your recipe.

39. Lemonade

The classic lemonade stand could still pay off, provided you don't spend more money making the drink than you make selling it. If you have access to free lemons from a tree or bush in your own yard, this helps cut down on your costs.

40. Salt-Free and/or Sugar-Free Meals

When someone must eat food containing no salt or no sugar, it becomes very difficult for them to figure out what to eat. Most frozen vegetables and frozen prepared meals have a great deal of salt and sugar in them. So do canned goods.

Often, people on these diets do not enjoy cooking for themselves, or are not able to do so. If you could find a way to prepare salt-free or sugar-free meals for such people, you might have lots of customers.

41. Popcorn

Popcorn is inexpensive if you pop it yourself, or if you buy it already popped in large bags like the ones theaters buy.

You could make a fairly large profit, if you could sell popcorn at neighborhood or church ball games, at tail-gate parties (before football games,) or some other function where there are crowds of people and where popcorn would be welcome.

You might be able to get permission to sell at certain functions, if you donate 10% of your proceeds to the organization sponsoring the event.

42. Pets

Raise hamsters, white mice, white rats, gerbils, rabbits, or fish, and sell them to pet stores.

If you have a purebred female dog with papers, you could consider raising puppies, but only if you can find a good male dog of the same breed, so the puppies could also be registered.

If you have a male purebred dog with a good pedigree, you could make money by having him father puppies for someone with a female of the same breed.

43. Toys

You could make dolls, teddy bears, other stuffed animals or toys, blocks, toy logs (from oak tree branches, walnut trees, or other trees), puzzles, and so-on.

Look in craft books and magazines for ideas and instructions. Go to craft stores or toy stores. Look for new ideas. Take craft classes.

44. Quiet Books For Children

You have probably seen the cloth books with a different activity on each page, such as a shoe with a shoelace that can be

Raise purebred puppies

laced and unlaced, or something to button and unbutton, or zip and unzip, braid, comb, or tie. You can design your own book or get ideas from somewhere else.

Quiet books can also be made out of brown paper bags (for pages) and pictures cut out of old magazines.

45. Craft Items

Quilts	Place Mats
Baby Blankets	Gingham Napkins
Baby Quilts	Aprons (Child or Adult)
Booties	Pot Holders
Wrapped Hangers	Dish Towels
Padded Picture Frames	Hats
Afghans	Mittens
Braided Rugs	Ponchos
Mobiles	Scarves
Belts	Pillows
Pet Toys	Bookmarks
Catnip Toys	Paper Weights

Eye Glass Cases	Pet Rocks
Jewelry	Bumper-Stickers
Note Paper	Tote Bags
Doll Clothes	Greeting Cards

To learn how to make some of these things, take classes, or learn from magazines or books. One good way to learn quilting, crocheting, knitting, embroidery, and several different crafts is by attending craft sessions held monthly by the Relief Society, which is a women's organization sponsored by The Church of Jesus Christ of LatterDay Saints, also known as the "Mormon Church." They are listed in the phone book. Call and ask for information about the Relief Society craft sessions, which they call, "work meetings." Visitors are welcome, and there is no charge.

46. More Craft Items

Necktie Rack	Paper-Towel Holder
Coat Rack	Neckties
Slippers, Knitted	Scarves
or Crocheted	Wooden "Milk Stools"
Silk Flowers	Small Purses with Long,
Other Artificial	Over-The-Shoulder Straps
Flowers	Handkerchiefs
Brocade, Upholstered	Doilies
Footstool	Bulletin Boards
Bean Bags	Hair Clips
Wooden Puzzles	Knickknack Shelves
Baby Clothes	Doll Houses
Hooded Towel Wrap	Small Easels for
for Babies	Pictures or Plates

47. Bake Sale

Hold a bake sale and sell cookies, candy, cakes, pies, and brownies.

48. Formal Dresses and Wedding Gowns

If you know how to sew and have access to a good sewing machine, formal dresses are not as difficult to make as it might

**Make wedding
gowns**

seem. It's the fabric that makes the difference. You can even make your own designs. Effective use of lace, sequins, beads, or other trimming will enhance your creation.

As you gain experience, you might decide to try wedding gowns.

Good fabric is expensive, and mistakes can be costly, so you should be confident of your abilities before undertaking large investments in material.

49. Sweat Suits

One of my sons plays tennis and has been making his own sweat suits or warm-up suits since he was a teen-ager. He makes original designs and wears them in tournament competition. They look like expensive, famous-brand outfits.

If he can do it, so can you.

50. Night Caps

Much of our body heat is lost through our scalps. At night, as the temperature cools down, we snuggle under the warm covers, but usually our heads are sticking out.

In the old days, when people had less efficient heating, they wore caps at night to keep warm. If we did this today, we could turn down the heat at night to save energy and still not "catch cold."

There aren't many such caps on the market at this time, but they are easy to make, and could be promoted as energy saving, health protecting items.

51. Magazines

Recycling centers don't usually take magazines. People who subscribe to several different "slick" magazines have to give them away or throw them out.

Collect these unwanted magazines and turn them over to someone who wants them, for a small "handling fee." To increase your inventory, you could offer to buy the magazines and still make a nice profit.

52. Care Baskets

If you live close to a college or university, you could prepare and deliver care baskets of fruit and vegetables, or soap, toothpaste and other basic necessities, or baskets of frivolity and fun with toys, games, jokes and balloons—to students who are living away from home. Devise a few different programs according to frequency, occasion (birthdays, holidays, etc.),and contents of the basket. Produce a brochure describing your Care Basket Program with its various options and prices and send it to out-of-town parents. They will subscribe to your service for their student "children."

Obtaining a mailing list might be a problem, but if necessary, you could offer to donate a percentage of your profits to the school, to a scholarship fund, or to a student organization.

53. Gift Baskets

Sell fancy fruit baskets for birthdays, "get well," or for holidays. Use fruit, cheese, nuts, vegetables, toys, or something unusual and attractive in keeping with the special theme. "Baskets" could be buckets, flower pots, fancy card-file boxes, or other attractive, practical containers. Dress them up with cellophane and bows.

You might be able to sell wholesale to a store or gift shop, if your product is good enough, and if you can meet the demand.

54. The Garage Sale

The first step in organizing a garage sale is gathering the merchandise. If one of your businesses is cleaning out other people's garages, attics, basements or yards, you will already have an inventory of useful items to include in your sale.

If you do not have this inventory, you must begin looking for things to sell. Your parents might have things they want to clean out of their closets, garage, basement, etc. Ask them if they are planning to do some cleaning and sorting soon, and tell them of your plans. You will need their permission, anyway—especially if you want to use their garage for storage and their driveway for the sale.

If you enjoy doing things with a friend, think about working as partners. When you have the actual sale, you will need help, so a partner would come in handy.

Next, go to your brothers and sisters. Do they have items they want to give away, throw away, or sell? You might offer to give them a percentage of what you make on their things.

Ask your neighbors if they have items they would like you to recycle for them. Again, you could offer to act as their agent and sell their things for a 25% commission on the price. Or you could offer to do two hours of yardwork or babysitting, or wash their car or do some other job in return for the items they give you.

If you do arrange to take merchandise on a percentage basis, you must keep good records. Assign each person a letter of the alphabet. In a clean notebook, label each page with the letters, beginning with "A." Under the first page, "A," you will write at the top the name, address, and phone number of the first person. Also write the percentage of commission you have agreed to charge or pay. Down the left side of the page, list and number each item they have given you to sell for them. If they have a minimum price they will accept for any of the items, enter that next to the item. Make a copy of this inventory and price list and give it to the person whose name is at the top of the page.

You will have to buy some peel-off labels to mark the merchandise. Label items you are selling for someone else by writing their assigned "letter" on the label, along with the number of the item and the price. For instance:

A-3
$4

As you sell each item, remove the sticker, place the sticker on the page for that person, and write the sale price in the last column next to the description of the item and the suggested price.

It is important to price and label things well before the sale, and to arrange small items on tables ahead of time so they can be quickly carried outside to the area where the sale will be held. If you can store things in the garage and move them out to the driveway the morning of the sale, this usually works well.

Your merchandise will sell faster and for a higher price, if you spend some time dusting, cleaning, and shining it.

Advertising. There are a few ways to advertise your garage sale at no cost. If it is legal in your town or city, you can post signs at key intersections, with your address and arrows pointing the way. These you would post the morning of the sale and remove right after the sale.

Some local newspapers allow free advertising for patrons or subscribers. They usually have a category for garage sales.

Signs on bulletin boards might work, depending on location.

Leaflets could be distributed downtown, if it is allowed. In our town it is not legal to leave leaflets on car windshields.

If you are on a busy street, a sign in front of your house might be enough to attract customers.

For a small fee, you can advertise in the local newspaper in the classified ad section under the heading, "garage sales."

Permits.   Some cities or towns require you to apply for a permit to have a garage sale. Usually these don't cost anything and you can get them at City Hall. However, there might be a fee, or even some rules. In our town, the permit costs $25.00 and there are lots of rules, including only one sale allowed per year. In the city next to us (two blocks away) a permit is required, but it is free and you can have as many sales as you want.

If you do have more than two or three sales in one year, the state might require you to collect sales tax.

The Sale.   On the day of the sale, you will get up very early to display your merchandise and post your signs.

One person should be seated at a card table with the cash box (plenty of change) and the notebook with inventories and records. This table should be placed so that no one can leave the sale without passing by it.

At least one other person should direct customers, answer questions, and mingle.

If you have worked hard, planned well, and the weather is good, you can make several hundred dollars on a successful garage sale, depending of course on the amount of merchandise you have been able to gather. If you have large items such as furniture, you could make even more.

As long as you are making the effort to organize, advertise, and hold a garage sale, you should also think about some other things you could sell there at the same time, such as popcorn, lemonade, seedlings you have started in small containers, house plants you have started from clippings, other plants you have gathered or started, or some of the craft items you have made.

55. Angora Wool

Raising Angora goats for their wool would be nice, but if this is not possible for you, try raising Angora rabbits. They take less space, and their long, soft fur can be harvested (without hurting the rabbits), spun into yarn, and used to make beautiful Angora garments.

Learn about dietary, temperature, and other requirements of the Angora rabbit before you decide to do this.

Charles and Henrietta
(My chickens had names.)

If you don't know how to spin the "wool" into yarn, you can sell the fur to someone who does.

56. Eggs

Raising chickens and selling their eggs is a possible money-making venture, provided you live in an area where this would not violate the local zoning regulations.

Rhode Island Red Hens lay beautiful, reddish-brown eggs with rich, dark-yellow yolks. Many people prefer these eggs to the white ones sold in grocery stores, and will pay more for them.

Health food stores might want to stock your eggs, if they know you are not feeding your chickens antibiotics or hormones.

57. Farm Animals

If you live on a farm or in the country, you have probably already thought about raising pigs, cows, horses, or other farm animals for profit.

Perhaps you are also a member of a local chapter of the 4-H Club, which helps young people learn about farming (and home-making) and sponsors competitive events related to these pursuits.

58. T-Shirts

Design clever logos or slogans for T-Shirts. Make them funny, based on the latest national or local bloopers in the news. (Johnny Carson does an excellent job of capitalizing on these things on The Tonight Show.) Or make them serious, to reflect a current popular cause or concern. Perhaps you could make shirts to go along with a school, city, state, or national campaign, if there is a hot issue or contest between candidates.

The main thing is to come up with shirts that will sell. If you can promote social awareness at the same time, that would be a definite bonus.

Test your ideas on your friends, to see which ones will sell, or try taking orders based on drawings. There are advantages to taking orders: customers can choose style, size, color, and logo, to come up with exactly what they want; and you won't have to risk stocking a huge inventory that might not sell.

Look in the Yellow Pages of your phone book under "T-Shirts" to find companies that specialize in making up custom, whole-sale shirts. Compare prices and selection. The more you order, the less the unit price.

You will have to make sure you can sell the shirts at a reasonable profit, but be careful not to buy more than you might sell, just to get a lower price per shirt.

Remember to allow some money for advertising, when you figure out your cost. After you get started, one good way to advertise would be to wear your product.

59. Bumper-Stickers and Buttons, etc.

Try the same clever slogans as bumper-stickers or buttons. Maybe different material would lend itself better to one form or the other. Try bookmarks. See if you can think of other vehicles for clever sayings. Notebook covers, book covers, pencils, hair-bobs, shoelaces, and handkerchiefs are good possibilities.

If you could manufacture the items yourself, you might make more money.

CHAPTER 7

GETTING PAID TWICE

It's always fun when you can get paid twice for your work. This could happen when you arrange for someone to pay you to remove from their property unwanted items, which you then sell.

Or it might be a case of taking care of something that can make money for you while you are taking care of it.

Make sure that what you plan to do with another person's property is all right with them.

For instance, if you are hired to drive a car from New York to Chicago, you must get permission to have someone else ride with you, either for a fee or for company.

The following money-making ideas could be examples of "getting paid twice."

1. Escargot (Snails)

Snails that are pests in the garden could be the same ones served as escargot by restaurants. Sometimes a restaurant will buy fresh snails from a local supplier. If you know where to find nice large, juicy snails, you could be that supplier.

Call some French restaurants and see if they would be interested in your snails. Find out how much they will pay. Ask them if they prefer to have you keep the snails for a certain period of time and feed them a particular diet.

Check with your County Health Department. See if they have any restrictions or rules about snails.

If you know someone with a terrible snail problem in their yard or garden, arrange for them to pay you a certain amount of

Snails can travel fast enough, when they're "making a getaway"

money for every snail you remove for them. Make sure they have
not been using any type of poison or snail bait. If so, you don't
want to think about selling their snails as food, although you
could still work at removing and destroying them.

The best time to harvest snails is either in the evening after
dark (hard to see) or early morning when the dew is still wet. A
light rain at night is great for snail hunting in the morning. On
one such occasion, I harvested over 200 snails in about 45
minutes.

Make sure you contain your snails in an escape-proof
enclosure that allows them to breathe. Snails are supposed to be
slow, but everything is relative. They can travel fast enough,
when they're "making a getaway."

2. Remove "Junk" and Sell It

If you are in the business of cleaning garages, basements,
attics, or yards, you could also be in the garage-sale business
and sell the unwanted items you have been paid to remove from
other people's homes and yards.

Before removing anything you think is junk, be sure to have the owner's approval.

3. Weeding and Seedling

When you come across volunteer seedlings while weeding, you could pot them instead of throwing them away. If you do this, it would not be fair to charge by the hour for your weeding.

After your seedlings have taken root, you can sell them at a garage sale or market them some other way.

4. Manure Versus Fertilizer

A job cleaning out horse stalls, chicken coops, rabbit hutches, or certain other animal pens presents you with an opportunity to start a fertilizer business. Mix the manure with sand, straw, or soil and sell this organic material to people with gardens. You should find out which kinds of manure are acceptable, how to mix it, and how to sterilize it against weeds.

5. Fruit and Nuts

If you are being paid to pick fruit or nuts, sometimes the owners do not want all of the produce. With their permission, you could take the extra fruit off their hands. This you would then sell.

6. Construction Clean-Up

On a construction site, there is always left-over scrap material that has to be picked up, swept out, and eventually hauled away to the dump. If you can get a job cleaning construction sites, get permission to remove things from the scrap pile (on your own time). This should save the contractor money, because it means less for him to haul away.

You can use select pieces of the scrap material to build some of your craft items. Other wood can be sold as kindling or firewood.

7. Mistletoe

Mistletoe is a parasite and can be harmful to trees, if there is too much of it. If you observe mistletoe taking over a large oak tree or some other tree (best seen in Fall or Winter when the tree loses its leaves), see if the owner will pay you to remove it.

Then package it in small plastic sandwich bags tied with red or green ribbon and sell it during the Christmas season. If you have enough, you could sell it wholesale to a store, or you could peddle it yourself.

One year my daughter and her girlfriend dressed up like elves and sold mistletoe door-to-door in office buildings. They had fun and made extra Christmas money at the same time.

8. Trim Trees

If your job is trimming trees, you could also sell the wood for firewood, if the owner wants it removed. You might use the branches and wood to make toys, furniture, or other craft projects.

If you are trimming certain evergreen trees just before Christmas, such as pine, juniper, or holly, you could make wreathes, or just tie a red bow on a few branches and sell them that way.

9. Weeds

Some weeds are edible. If you know how to recognize them, you could harvest and market them when you run into a good, healthy batch while weeding for someone.

Dandelion greens picked from first year's growth before the flowering stalks have formed make good greens for salad. Miner's Lettuce, Mustard Greens, and Curly Dock are also good when used properly.

Go to the library and look for pictures of edible "weeds." Study their uses and how and when to pick them.

Be careful not to use weeds that have been exposed to animal feces or harmful chemicals, such as those used to kill weeds or bugs.

Chapter 8

JOURNALISM, SPORTS, AND THE ARTS

1. Newspaper Column

Write a column for a newspaper. It could be humorous, informative, or newsy. Possibly it could be an advice column for kids or teens. First, write several pieces, then submit them to different newspapers until you find a paper that needs your column.

2. Write a Book or Story

A children's book might be a good place to start, although children's stories aren't necessarily easy just because they are for a young age group. If you like to read and are good at writing, you could try to create the type of story or non-fiction article you most enjoy.

3. Family Newsletter

I'm not sure how you could make money writing a family newsletter, unless you could get members of your distant family to subscribe, or unless you could include ads of some sort from different family members.

4. Neighborhood Newsletter

This would be fun for residents of your neighborhood, and they would probably be happy to subscribe, if it is good.

People like to see their own names or names of their children in print. The more names you include in your publication, the more copies you will sell.

You also might be able to sell advertising space to local businesses or local professional people, such as insurance or real estate agents.

5. Community Newspaper

The Community Newspaper would include a larger area than the Neighborhood Newsletter, and would be a more serious commitment. It presents a greater potential for making money, which will come from advertisers and not subscribers. You can sell more advertising if you have a large circulation. The way to increase circulation is to give the paper to everyone in the community.

You should have some training and experience in journalism and have some co-workers with similar credentials before attempting to publish a Community Newspaper.

6. Broadcasting

Just as you might have a newspaper column, you might also be able to have a radio program, or a spot on a program.

7. Video Productions

There are several possibilities for the person with access to video equipment. You can record important events like birthday parties, speeches, weddings, anniversaries, or bar mizvah celebrations.

You could also make artistic video films, movies, or ads.

8. Films

Short subject films would be fun to produce, and if they are good enough, you might find a market for them directly or through an agent.

9. Sports Instructor

If you are good at tennis, swimming, soccer, gymnastics, or some other sport, you could offer to teach others.

This might affect your amateur status, so if you are participating in competition, you should find out what the regulations are. You don't want to disqualify yourself by turning professional without realizing it.

10. Paintings and Sculpture

You will be able to sell some of your work, if you are gifted. Sometimes a less talented student of art will have more commercial success by paying attention to the market and producing the kind of art people are buying.

11. Ceramics

Creating practical and fanciful ceramic objects could be profitable, if you have a retail outlet for your work.

12. Teaching Art

The same applies to art as to sports and music, except that it might be more difficult to find individual students. Perhaps you could assist in community center art classes.

13. Body Painting

How would you market this? Set up a stand? Advertise? This is certainly the era for body painting, if you could find a way to attract customers.

14. Sign Painting

Real Estate Brokers and other small businesses need signs, as do larger businesses. You could also offer personalized signs to individuals. "Allergy, No Smoking Please," or "Please Park Here," are examples of often needed, yet hard to find signs.

15. Drama

Write and produce a play. This is a large undertaking, but can be a lot of fun.

"Remember F-Sharp"

16. Musical Performing Group

You could organize a band or a singing group and play or perform for dances and community events.

17. Dance

If you are not a solo performer, you could have a team of dancers, work out routines, and perform at different functions or on TV.

18. Teach Music or Dancing

It is not unusual for gifted or fairly advanced students of music or dance to teach beginners and intermediate students.

19. Painted Rocks

Paint small, medium, or large rocks. Make them colorful, intricate, imaginative, or true-to-life. Invent fanciful creatures, or make the rocks look like real animals, people, or objects, depending on the natural shape of each rock.

Recently, while browsing in a small shop, I saw a good-sized gray rock painted to look like a sleeping tabby cat. It was priced over $200.

CHAPTER 9

HOLIDAYS

Certain projects do better during various holiday seasons, and some are only appropriate for a specific holiday, as with Christmas tree ornaments.

A few of the following ideas have been mentioned earlier and are repeated here for easy holiday reference.

NEW YEAR'S EVE

1. Confetti

Can you think of a way to make confetti out of old magazines, scrap paper, or junk mail? A shredding machine might be helpful.

2. Party Decorations

Make and sell appropriate decorations and party favors.

3. Decorating Service

Offer a decorating service for parties.

4. Clean-Up Service

A party clean-up service should be very welcome after New Year's Eve celebrations.

VALENTINE'S DAY

1. Live Valentines

Offer different imaginative Valentine greetings, to be delivered, sung, or acted out in person.
Costumes make this more interesting.

2. Greeting Cards

If you have your own ideas for cards, this and other holidays would present logical opportunities.

EASTER

1. Eggs

How about an Easter Egg decorating service?

2. Easter Bunny

Rent yourself out as an Easter Bunny (complete with costume, of course).

3. Easter Bonnets

Create Easter Bonnets out of straw hats by adding flowers, scarves, or ribbons.

FOURTH OF JULY

1. Performing

The Fourth of July is a good time to perform, if you have a musical group or a dance team.

2. Decorations and Clean-Up

This is another opportunity to make decorations, to decorate, and to clean up afterward.

Custom costumes

HALLOWEEN

1. Haunted House

Dream up and execute a spooky haunted house. Charge admission.

2. Costumes

Make "custom costumes" for children or adults.

3. Pumpkins

Pumpkins are easy to grow in your garden. Begin now to harvest and sell them, along with Indian Corn or any dried corn stalks you might also have.

4. Escort Service

An escort service for young "Trick-Or-Treaters" would be helpful to parents. You could escort several children at the same time, making it possible to charge a reasonable fee and yet make a worthwhile profit.

THANKSGIVING

1. Bake Sales

Hold bake sales now, while everyone has their mind on food. Also, you could sell any left-over pumpkins from your garden, as well as dried flowers.

2. Pies To Order

Develop your pie-making skills ahead of time. Choose the tastiest recipes (especially for pumpkin pie), and take orders. Deliver the day before or on Thanksgiving Day, if possible.

CHRISTMAS

1. Pinecones

Collect and sell pinecones.

2. Decorations

Make original tree ornaments, wreaths, Christmas card holders, and other holiday decorations.

3. Gingerbread Houses

Gingerbread Houses probably sell best at this time of year.

4. Stockings

Make Christmas stockings of your own design.

5. Holly and Mistletoe, etc.

During the Christmas season there is a demand for holly, mistletoe, and evergreen boughs.

Make
Christmas
Tree
ornaments

6. Addressing Service

Many people feel overwhelmed at the thought of addressing Christmas cards, especially if their list is long. Some senior citizens would like to send cards, but are not able to address them.

Offer a Christmas card addressing service.

7. Gift Wrapping

Wrapping gifts for people in their own homes would be a helpful way to make money.

8. Gift Service

It would take a lot of hectic pressure out of the holiday season for busy people, if they hire you to assist them with their shopping.

9. Bazaar

December is the perfect month to hold a bazaar to sell the many craft items you have made throughout the year, as well as the Christmas things mentioned in this section.

10. Package Wrapping and Mailing Service

Pick up, wrap for mailing, and mail packages for people. This would include standing in lines at the Post Office.

CHAPTER 10

A WIDER DAY

There are fewer limits to the amount of money you can make when you are *not* working for a fixed salary. Working by the hour for someone else restricts the amount you can earn. Unless you are a doctor, lawyer, plumber, or electrician, etc., you might find it hard to live on an hourly wage or fee. Working for commissions can sometimes be very rewarding—or not so rewarding, depending on how much you are able to sell.

If you are relying solely on what you can do by yourself, you will soon notice that there are not enough hours in a day.

Two girls who are sharing an apartment work for six and seven dollars an hour. With two jobs each, working by the hour they cannot make enough to pay their bills.

We must accept the fact that one day consists of exactly twenty-four hours. Thirty years from now this will probably still be true. One day = 24 hours.

My father used to say, "The days are plenty long. They're just not *wide* enough!" Dad was a busy, energetic man with lots of creativity. It frustrated him to come to the end of a long, tiring day without accomplishing everything he wanted to do.

So, it seems the solution to our problem is not to make the days longer, but to make them wider. How? Start thinking in terms of an enterprise that will make money, even if you are not there to run it all the time.

For instance:

1. Renting

Rent something you own, such as a house, a room in a house, an apartment, a car, a boat, a rototiller, an evening gown, costumes, books, computer time, bicycles, or garden tools.

2. Lending

Lend money and charge interest (usually monthly). Find out about current federal and state fair lending laws, and be careful to obey them.

3. Notes

Sell something you own and take an interest-bearing note as part of the payment. Again, check the fair lending laws.

4. Employees

Pay someone else to work for you, such as a manager, a salesman, or people to help perform the services you offer.

There are many things to remember when you have employees. Social Security tax, withholding state and federal income tax, and insurance are all an employer's responsibility. It would be wise to consult a good accountant to help you conform to these and other laws or regulations.

5. Value Growth

Buy things that increase in value as time passes. Real estate, antiques, and works of art are good examples. These are usually long-term investments, but it is better to spend your money on them than on other things that go out of style or quickly decrease in value after you buy them, such as fashionable clothes, cars, new furniture, gadgets, hi-fi's, compact disc players, television sets, and other electronic equipment. There are lots of people who have the latest in everything, but never have any money.

6. Investments

Invest in bonds, stocks, money markets, precious metals, or foreign currency. All of these have some degree of risk—some more than others. It is important to have a good broker who will listen to your needs and goals, then help you buy what is best for you.

7. Vending Machines

Buy or lease vending machines, video games, pinball machines, juke boxes, or coin-operated washers and driers. Place them in safe, monitored locations to avoid vandalism and theft.

8. Perpetual Rewards

Arrange to be paid again and again for something you have already done. Authors and inventors get royalties. Actors get residuals. Insurance agents get renewal commissions. Think about it.

9. Savings Account

Don't forget your savings program. Once you are in the habit of saving regularly, your money will earn interest for you and grow by itself.

Refer back to the discussion on saving regularly, in Chapter 2.

PART THREE

HELPFUL HINTS

Now that you are thinking clearly about your future financial security, have set some goals, and are considering a few different ways to make money, *what next?*

This section offers many suggestions to help you succeed in your business venture.

You must ask yourself whether or not your business requires some money to get started. If so, how much? Where can you get it?

How will you attract your first customers? How do you keep them coming back? Should you advertise?

How can you avoid common costly mistakes?

Finally—what is success? Are you *ready* for success? Will you recognize it?

Keep reading . . .

How can you succeed in your business venture?

Chapter 11

GOOD BUSINESS

There are a few simple things you can do to make your business successful. Because these common-sense rules are so obvious, many people underestimate their importance and fail to follow them consistently. I urge you not to make that mistake.

COMMON-SENSE RULES OF GOOD BUSINESS

1. BE DEPENDABLE AND ON TIME

This rule is broken regularly by most independent contractors I know. They make promises to be on the job at a certain time or on a given day and are either two to four hours late, or never show up at all. This happens often and is very frustrating for the customer.

In order to be better than most of the competition, all you have to do is be on time. Never make promises you might not be able to keep, or worse yet, have no intention of keeping.

2. PAY YOUR BILLS PROMPTLY

This is as important in your business as it is in your personal life. People who supply you with material or services appreciate getting paid promptly. If you make this a habit, you will be given special consideration. When you have unusual needs or short notice, people won't mind helping you, if they can.

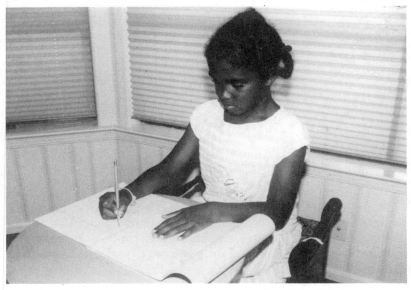

Keep good records

Paying bills late is not only inconsiderate, but it is costly. Why pay late fees or interest, and risk ruining your good credit rating as well?

3. KEEP GOOD RECORDS

Believe it or not, many businesses fail because they don't realize they are losing money, until it is too late. Why? Because they don't keep good records.

When you sell a product or a service, you must be aware of the total cost to you, or you could easily lose money.

You must consider your overhead. Overhead is the cost of renting office space, utilities, insurance, equipment, vehicles, maintenance of equipment and vehicles, gas, cost of employee benefits, the cost of accounting, and so-on.

Also, remember the cost of materials, inventory, and labor.

Without good records and a good overall picture of the cost of doing business, you could think that because you are taking in money, you are making money.

4. BE HONEST AND TREAT EVERYONE FAIRLY

This includes both your customers and people working for you.

If you don't pay your workers a fair share or wage, they will be resentful and might find ways to even up the score. If you are generous and thoughtful, your employees should be loyal and productive.

It is good business to give your customers good value for their money. Give them more than their money's worth, when you can. Guarantee your service or your product. If the product doesn't work, fix it or give the customer a refund. If your service was not satisfactory, do it again, or make it right.

5. BE PLEASANT AND COURTEOUS

For something that costs so little, being pleasant and courteous brings big dividends.

Few people remember to do this as much as they should. Sometimes you just don't feel like being pleasant. Do it anyway. Soon you will feel good, and so will your customer.

The pleasant, courteous bid might win over a lower bid. This has been my personal experience, both as a salesman and as a customer.

6. REMEMBER, THE CUSTOMER IS *ALWAYS* RIGHT

Even when they're wrong, they are right. You have little to gain by arguing with the customer. Their satisfaction is what counts.

This does not mean you will sell them what they say they want, if you know it won't give them the results they need. You can explain what you feel they should have, based on your knowledge, without making them feel wrong or stupid.

7. KEEP IN TOUCH WITH YOUR CUSTOMERS

One of the best sources for new jobs, sales, or business is past customers and referrals from past customers.

If you have provided the type of service that is a recurring need, keep a calendar file, so you can call your customers before they require the service again. Washing windows, rototilling, pruning, fertilizing service, and painting are examples of this.

You could send seasonal greeting cards, or remember their birthdays or some other special occasion.

The best way to get a referral is to ask for one. Include this in a follow-up card or call. Ask if your service was satisfactory, and ask if they have any friends who might be needing the service you offer.

8. DRESS FOR SUCCESS

You will be amazed when you find out what miracles will happen when you are "dressed for success." It is more than being properly dressed. Dressing for success is almost an exact science.

John T. Molloy has written two books on this subject. The first is for men: *Dress for Success*. The second, *The Woman's Dress for Success Book,* is for women. Both are available in paperback and published by Warner Books.

9. RESEARCH THE MARKET BEFORE YOU BEGIN

Don't overdo this. If your business is simple, just try it and see. If you do some of the other things in this chapter, you could be successful, even if others have already failed in the same venture.

It is still a good idea to size up the competition and the market.

Cost research is very important. If you can't deliver the service or product at a reasonable cost, you might not have any customers, unless they are willing to pay more for the extra quality you can provide.

Dress for success

10. FIND OUT IF YOU NEED A PERMIT OR LICENSE

Check with the county and the city in which you will be operating. A special permit or license might be required. See if they have any rules or regulations that will apply to you.

11. LEARN ABOUT INSURANCE

Talk to your parents and their insurance agent. Find out if you and your business will be covered by their existing homeowner's and liability policy. Do you need additional insurance, such as Errors and Omissions, Theft, or Liability? If so, by all means, get it.

A friend of mine opened a jewelry store. He didn't buy insurance, because it was "too expensive." His little store was robbed, and the thief took about $30,000 worth of gold jewelry. Most of his merchandise was in the store on consignment, so my friend had to pay his supplier for the stolen jewelry. This cost him his house, since he didn't have $30,000. Do you think the insurance would have been a good investment?

12. LOOK FOR WAYS TO LOWER YOUR COST OF DOING BUSINESS

In other words, "A penny saved is a penny earned."

Always be on the lookout for ways to lower your overhead and the cost of your supplies. Analyze your operation. Can you be more efficient with your material or your time?

Don't sacrifice quality, unless your product or service is actually a higher quality than is necessary. For instance, there is "finish quality" and "rough quality" in the building trade. It is usually pointless to use "finish quality" work and materials on an outside fence. The cost would be outrageous.

13. DO WHAT OTHERS ARE NOT DOING

Following the crowd is easy, but not always smart. This is true of many things in life, and it is true in business.

When real estate prices are high, people buy. When the prices are low, they sell. Does this make sense? The same thing is true of the stock market. People get frightened and stampede to their own destruction.

Learn to think for yourself.

You might even come up with profitable innovations in your business, if you are not afraid of being different.

14. NEVER USE PROFANITY, SMOKE, CHEW GUM (OR TOBACCO), OR PLAY A RADIO WHILE YOU ARE WITHIN EARSHOT OR IN THE PRESENCE OF YOUR CUSTOMER

These habits can only hurt your professional image and possibly interfere with your success. Why risk alienating a customer unnecessarily?

Today, using the Lord's name "in vain" is a common practice. It is a form of profanity that is particularly offensive to many people, and it should be carefully avoided.

Playing a radio while you work in someone else's home or in their yard is usually annoying to others who can hear it. If they had wanted to listen to the radio, they would be doing so. People resent having their homes invaded by sounds they don't enjoy, or which interfere with their concentration. This is a mistake made by many workers, who often make elaborate preparations to ensure that they will have their brand of music available to them while they work. They might forget their tools, but they never forget their radio and stereo speakers.

If you have a shop where your customers come to you, the same rules apply. Be very careful not to have jarring, loud, contemporary music playing throughout the store. It will drive some customers away.

The smell of smoke will also cause some people not to stay, and possibly never to come back. Do not smoke or allow others to smoke in your store.

It pays to give careful consideration to everything that affects your customer's comfort and mood.

15. THINK TWICE ABOUT WEARING COLOGNE OR PERFUME

Be very careful about wearing cologne or perfume. What smells good to you might be offensive to or trigger an allergy in someone else. People who are sensitive to odors will — out of self-preservation — make it a point not to be in your presence again, if they can help it.

If the fragrance smells good to your customer, they could get the wrong message.

Think twice about wearing cologne or perfume.

16. ENJOY WHAT YOU ARE DOING

If you find enjoyment and satisfaction in your work, you will be healthy, happy, and successful.

A sure way to find satisfaction in your work is to concentrate on helping people. Do a good job for the customer. Take pride in the finished product.

Enjoy your work

When I was selling real estate, I always felt best when I could help someone buy their first house or their first investment property. It took longer, because first-time buyers need a lot of encouragement, explanation, and education, and usually they don't have much money. I enjoyed the creative challenge of accomplishing the "impossible."

CHAPTER 12

FINANCING YOUR BUSINESS

Many businesses, such as baby sitting, tutoring, pet walking, weeding, or picking pests, have the advantage of requiring little or no initial investment to get started—unless you find it necessary to spend money on advertising and promotion.

Other businesses, like lawn care, rototilling, painting, or cleaning, cannot be started without equipment, material, or supplies. Unless you borrow the things you need, you will have to buy them.

If you have your heart set on a business that costs money, and you have none, there are several things you can do to realize your dream.

1. Earning Your Own Capital

You might consider working at one of the "no-equipment-required" professions until you earn enough to start the kind of business you really want.

(This is a lot like buying a house you don't want, but can afford, so you can at a later time afford to buy the house you *do* want. Too many people fail to buy their first house, year after year, because they won't settle for anything less than the perfect house in a perfect location.)

2. Borrowing From Your Parents

Arrange a business loan with your parents. Write down the terms of the loan, including interest, the amount you owe, and

Some businesses require an initial investment in equipment

how you will pay it back. Make the payment plan realistic, so you can stick to it. Sign the note, use the money wisely, work hard, and live up to the bargain you have made with your parents.

Never take advantage of your parents' generosity and good intentions. That would weaken your own self respect, and eventually destroy your credit with the most important back-up system you would otherwise have had available to you for years to come.

Show your parents how much you appreciate their confidence in you by succeeding in your business, and by paying back the money you borrowed, as agreed. Even if your business does not live up to your expectations right away, do another kind of work, so you can make your loan payments on time.

3. Small Business Loans or Grants

Find out about small business loans and grants available from the government. These loans are usually given with very generous terms, including low interest.

Request information on Small Business Loans by writing to:

Director, Office of Business Loans
Small Business Administration
1441 L Street, NW
Washington, DC 20416

Go to the library and research other sources of loans or grants. Depending on your own particular situation, such as family income, race, national origin, or the nature of your new business, you could be eligible for any number of loans, grants, or other types of assistance.

The book, *Getting Yours,* by Matthew Lesko, describes many sources of money and tells you how and where to apply. It is an informative guide for someone who needs money to start a business, get an education, do research, provide a service, or finance a special project.

4. Bank Loans

Banks have many different ways of lending money. There are programs associated with checking accounts, which are called by various different names, such as, "Checking-Plus." This allows you to borrow money from a previously approved credit line (up to a certain limit), simply by writing checks for more than the balance in your checking account.

Another program, called "Capital Advantage" in one bank, is a credit line set up as a separate account, against which you write checks as you need the money. There is usually an annual fee of about $45 for this type of credit line, whether you use it or not. However, the interest is tied to the Prime Rate, or some other index, and is fair. Also, the interest is not charged until you use the money, and then only on the amount borrowed.

The best way to find out about bank loans is to shop around. Visit several banks. Explain your needs and ask what types of loans are available.

5. Credit Cards

Using credit cards to borrow money is not a good idea, unless they start charging less interest.

6. Partnerships

If your business would be more successful with two people working together, and if you need help raising money to get started, choose a partner who can help financially. Of course, this partner should qualify in other ways, such as experience, skill, temperament, and honesty.

If you want to work alone, but need financial backing, you could arrange for a "silent partner," whose contribution to the business would be to provide that backing. Think twice about doing this, though. You might not want to create a permanent relationship where the other person shares in your profits forever, just because you needed a little money to get started. Only as a last resort would you do this in a small business. It's usually smarter just to borrow the money or earn it yourself, or start smaller than you would if you had more money.

Chapter 13

ADVERTISING YOUR BUSINESS

Advertising your business is a creative undertaking, and can be a lot of fun, as well as a challenge. There are several ways to promote your venture that cost nothing, other ways that involve some cost, and of course there are more expensive ways to advertise.

NO COST

1. Free Ads

Some local papers, circulars, newsletters, or trade publications have sections for free classified ads. In our area, the Palo Alto Weekly and a real estate newsletter are examples of this. You might have to be a subscriber or member, in order to be eligible for the free ads.

2. Spread the Word

"Word of mouth" is often very effective. Talk about your new business. Make sure your friends know. Contact people who might know others who could be interested in what you have to offer.

3. Good Will

Do an outstanding job for your customers, and you will get repeat business from them.

4. Referrals

Ask for referrals. When you have given good service or value to someone, ask that customer if they know anyone who could use your service or product.

5. New Release

Write an interesting "news release" about your new business and send it to local papers. Newspapers are always looking for news, and if they like your article, they will print it. They might even decide to do a longer, feature article on you and your business.

6. Telephone Soliciting

Depending on the nature of your enterprise, you might find it helpful to try telephone soliciting. If you have access to a reverse directory, you will be able to call people according to address. This way you can control the distance you have to travel between appointments.

7. Community Exposure

Offer to do volunteer work at community events. This will enable you to meet more people and give them a chance to get acquainted with you.

8. Ads for a Commission

If you are selling a product instead of offering a service, there is another way to advertise at no initial cost. Contact clubs or organizations that publish newsletters, bulletins, or circulars. See if they will advertise your product in their publication and/or promote it at their meetings in return for a mutually agreeable commission on all sales they generate.

Choose organizations that have members who could logically be interested in your product. For instance, if you are selling a new, handy garden tool, garden clubs would be a good place to start. If your product is for children, try the PTA or another parent support group.

Make sure you know how you can supply enough products to meet the expected (or unexpected) demand.

SOME COST

1. Classified Ads

Place an ad in the classified section of your local newspaper. There should be a special featured space for services. If you are offering yardwork, for instance, you would do well to list your ad there.

Study the classified section. Notice the different categories. Look at the appearance and wording of the other ads. What attracts your eye?

When you call to place your ad, you can specify exactly how you want each line to read. If you want your lines centered, tell them. Often it is helpful to have some blank space around your ad, if other ads don't. You can do this by centering and using fewer words on each line.

Words like, "courteous," "dependable," and "prompt," will usually impress a prospective client or customer. The term, "experienced," is good to use, if it applies to you.

2. Business Cards

Business cards are nice to have and are a form of advertising. You can give them to people when you talk to them about your business, so they will have easy access to your phone number when they need your service.

You could leave some of your cards in paint stores, if you are a painter, a garden center, if you offer gardening services, or in a sprinkler supply house, if your business is installing sprinklers, and so on. It might be useful to leave a few of your cards at banks, offices, or other businesses, if you can get permission to do so.

3. Stationery

Letterhead stationery is fairly reasonable in cost. It gives you a more professional image and tells people you are serious about what you are doing.

If you include in your letterhead an abbreviated suggestion of what your business offers, it can serve as another advertising tool. For instance, if you have a plant feeding service, you could say,

Fred's Fertilizing Service
For Lawns, Flowers, and Fruit Trees
Fred Smith
1234 Maple Lane • Anywhere, California 94000

4. Posters

Posters nicely done and cleverly worded could be a part of your advertising campaign, depending on your business.

5. Fliers

Fliers are a fast way to reach a lot of people locally. Make sure they are legal in your city. Leaving fliers on windshields is not permitted in our town, because they tend to create instant litter.

6. Cooperative Advertising

Join with friends in different businesses, and promote several services or products in one large ad, in a circular, or with fliers. This increases everyone's exposure for less money.

7. Ads in Local Publications

Advertising in your local high school newspaper, or in a church directory is fairly inexpensive and could bring good results.

GREATER COST

1. Display Ads

Display ads in the newspaper are costly, but you might try it for some special promotion. If you collaborate with friends in other businesses, it becomes more reasonable.

2. Magazine Ads

Ads in national magazines are very expensive and only seem wise for a large promotional effort, such as direct order advertising.

You can obtain rates for different magazines by writing to the Advertising Department at the address listed toward the front of the magazine with names of editors and other departments.

3. Billboards

Billboard space doesn't cost as much as you might expect, depending on the location.

Look in the Yellow Pages under "Advertising, Outdoor," or under "Signs," or look in the index to the Yellow Pages under "Billboard Advertising."

4. Yellow Pages

A listing in the Yellow Pages of your telephone book is an excellent way to advertise your business, if you expect to be working full-time and year-round.

CHAPTER 14

TWELVE THINGS
TO REMEMBER

1. Enjoy your work.
2. Be friendly.
3. Be enthusiastic and cheerful.
4. Dress for success.
5. Treat others fairly.
6. Be dependable.
7. Obey laws.
8. Keep good records.
9. Know income tax laws.
10. Set goals.
11. Dream.
12. Have the courage to act out your dream.

AVOID TWELVE COMMON COSTLY MISTAKES

1. Slow response to your customer's initial attempt to contact you

2. Arriving late

3. Failing to pay bills early or on time

4. Losing your temper

5. Forgetting to keep in touch with your customers

6. Not analyzing your operation periodically, to find ways to lower your costs

7. Using profanity, tobacco, or chewing gum

8. Forcing customers to listen to your radio in their own homes, or to loud, possibly objectionable music in your place of business

9. Wearing cologne or perfume

10. Following the crowd

11. Negative self-talk

12. Failing to make your money work for you

CHAPTER 16

BOOKS TO OWN
AND READ OFTEN

1. *How To Win Friends and Influence People,* by Dale Carnegie.
2. *Dress for Success,* by John T. Molloy.
3. *The Woman's Dress for Success Book,* by John T. Molloy.
4. *Your Income Tax,* by J. K. Lasser (Revised annually.)
5. A good dictionary, such as: *The American College Dictionary,* or *Webster's New Collegiate Dictionary.*

CHAPTER 17

SUCCESS

The road to success is a roadway meant to be well-traveled by many young people enthusiastically working out their own financial independence — in addition to other precious goals. (Remember, money should not be the only goal in life. True joy comes from other things discussed in Chapter One, many of which are better achieved if one is financially secure.)

We cannot travel down this roadway by sitting around, waiting for a successful parent or other member of the family to do something for us — or worse yet, die and make us rich.

My grandmother was a good businesswoman. She had a long, successful career as a chiropractor (retiring in her late 70's), and had the good sense to invest in residential rental property early-on. As a widowed mother of six children, security was very important to her. She planned for her children's education and for her own financial independence.

Her children were in their 60's and 70's when she died at age 99, having spent her nest egg in her old age. What would their lives have been like, had they been waiting to inherit their mother's estate?

Success is not perfection or beating out the competition. You don't have to be better than everyone else in order to succeed, but you do have to make a good personal effort.

I spent the first 35 years of my life trying to be the best — trying to get straight A's in school, trying to run faster and jump higher, trying to play the piano better than my friends, and trying to raise perfect children and have a perfect marriage. Sometimes I succeeded for awhile, but often, I fell short of my own expectations.

Eventually, I began to understand that I could be happy with myself if I put forth the best effort possible for me at any given time, taking into account other circumstances in my life over which I had little control.

This is not to say that you and I shouldn't try to be the best we can be. We should. But we must realize that when we do our best, that is enough. We can rejoice in the achievements and excellence of others freely, without feeling threatened or inadequate.

It is actually possible for *everyone* to be the best they can be. In fact, that is what life is about, and the sooner we realize it, the sooner we can enjoy the fruits of our own efforts and the accomplishments of our friends.

WHAT IS SUCCESS?

• Success is being kind and helping each other.

• Sucess is apprecieating our beautiful world, enjoying nature, and loving life.

• Sucess is starting over as many times as it takes, until you get it right.

• Success doesn't wait for us at the end of the road. It is all around us, as we journey. Watch for it. Stop. Look. Reach out. Touch it. Don't pass it by.

YOU DESERVE TO SUCCEED.

DO IT.

GOOD LUCK

You are on your way to

FINANCIAL SUCCESS and PERSONAL SECURITY.

INDEX

ORDER FORM

Calico Paws Publishing
Marketing Department
Post Office Box 2364-A
Menlo Park, CA 94026-2364

You may order more copies of KIDS CAN MAKE MONEY TOO! at the following prices and discount prices:

1 book . . . . $9.95 plus $1.10 shipping

2–9 books . . . . 8.96 ea. plus .65 ea. shipping

10–49 books . . . . 7.96 ea. plus .45 ea. shipping

Number of books, _____x $_____ ea. = _____

Plus Sales Tax for Californians: 6½% = _____

Plus Shipping, _____books x _____ea. = _____

Total Enclosed = _____

Name: _____

Address: _____

_____ Zip: _____

Organization: _____Phone: _____

If you are interested in larger quantities to use as a fund-raising project, please write for further details. Large orders are available at greater discounts. Include the name of your organization, and the name, address, and phone number of the person you wish us to contact.

ORDER FORM
T-Shirts, Sweat Shirts, Night Shirts, Aprons and Tote-Bags

Also available, KIDS CAN MAKE MONEY TOO! Tee Shirts, Night-Shirts, Sweat Shirts, Aprons, and Tote Bags. Attractive and FUN!

T-Shirts: Small Calico Paws Logo appears on the left side of the front of the shirt, and reproduction of *Kids Can Make Money Too!* cover is on the back of the shirt.

100% cotton, pre-shrunk, creamy beige $11.95

Small (34-36), Medium (38-40), Large (42-44), X-Large (46-48).

(Please indicate sizes and how many.)

Sweat Shirts: Small Calico Paws Logo appears on the left side of the front of the shirt, and reproduction of *Kids Can Make Money Too!* cover is on the back of the shirt. 50% Polyester, 50% Cotton, beige $19.95

Small (34-36), Medium (38-40), Large (42-44), X-Large (46-48).

(Please indicate sizes and how many.)

Night Shirts: 100% cotton, one-size fits all $18.95

Available in aqua.

Reproduction of *Kids Can Make Money Too!* cover appears on the front of the night-shirt.

Quantity ordered _____.

Aprons: Natural canvas, with reproduction of *Kids Can Make Money Too!* cover on front of apron.
27" long x 28½" wide. Two pockets $14.95

Tote Bags: Natural canvas, 10½" x 14½" with reproduction of *Kids Can Make Money Too!* cover on front $13.95

MAKE CHECK PAYABLE TO: *Calico Paws Publishing.* Please add $1.10 per item for shipping, and 6½% sales tax, if you live in California.

Mail To:		
Calico Paws Publishing	Amount of order	$_____
Marketing Department	Sales Tax, 6½%	+_____
Post Office Box 2364-A	Shipping	+_____
Menlo Park, CA 94026-2364	Total Enclosed	_____

Name _____

Address _____

_____ Zip: _____

Phone _____

If you are not satisfied, you may return any items within 60 days for a full refund.

ONE MORE WAY
TO MAKE MONEY...

... Become a distributor for *Kids Can Make Money Too!* books, T-shirts, sweat shirts, night-shirts, aprons, and tote bags (as described on the two preceding pages), plus other books and items as they become available.

Calico Paws would like to have at least one enthusiastic, dependable young (or young at heart) representative in every community. You would visit bookstores in your area at regular intervals to supply them with books as needed.

As on independent contractor, you could develop your own marketing strategy. This might include participating in fairs, art shows, and boutiques, or school and community fund raising events. You could advertise with brochures, fliers, posters, or notices on bulletin boards.

You're the boss. You decide how much money you will make. Set your own goals. Make your own promotional plan. Be creative.

For further details and an application form, write to:

Calico Paws
Distribution
Post Office Box 2364-A
Menlo Park, CA 94026-2364